Opportunities

Beginner

Contents

1	Hello	2
2	Meet the family	8
3	At home	14
4	At school	20
5	Going out	26
6	Playing sport	32
7	Every day	38
8	Free time	44
9	Excursions	50
10	Wildlife	56
11	Memories	62
12	At night	68
13	Accidents	74
14	Missing home	80
15	Tests	86
16	Goodbye	92
	Character Profiles	98
	Dictionary Quiz	100
	Key Word Bank	101
	Mini-Grammar	105

Language Powerbook

Longman

1 Hello

1 GRAMMAR
I am/you are, What?/Where? my/your

1 ★ *I am/you are*
Write sentences with full forms.

1 I/Italy
   I am from Italy.
2 You/Poland
   ....
3 I/New York
   ....
4 You/Australia
   ....
5 I/London
   ....
6 You/Britain
   ....

2 ★ *I am not/you are not*
Write sentences with full forms.

1 I/not/Russia.
   I am not from Russia.
2 You/not/Australia
   ....
   ....
3 I/not/Buenos Aires
   ....
   ....
4 You/not/Canada
   ....
   ....
5 I/not/Athens
   ....
   ....
6 You/not/the United States
   ....
   ....

3 ★★ **Affirmative and negative: Short forms**
Now write the sentences in Exercises 1 and 2 with short forms.

1 I/Italy. I/not/Russia.
   I'm from Italy. I'm not from Russia.
2 ....
3 ....
4 ....
5 ....
6 ....

4 ★★ **Questions and short answers**
Write the questions and complete the short answers.

1 you/Canada
   Are you from Canada? Yes, *I am.*
2 you/Istanbul
   ....? No, ...
3 you/Warsaw
   ....? Yes, ...
4 you/Australia
   ....? No, ...
5 you/St Petersburg
   ....? Yes, ...
6 you/Argentina
   ....? No, ...

5 ★ *What/Where* **questions and answers**
Write the words in the correct order.

1 I'm/Hi!/Jennifer.
   Hi! I'm Jennifer.
2 name?/What's/your
   ....
3 you/from?/are/Where
   ....
4 Anna./My/name's
   ....
5 Rome./from/I'm
   ....

Hello 1

6 ★ I/my, you/your
Circle the correct word.

Kate: Hello. (1) *I'm*/*My* Kate. What's (2) *you*/*your* name?
Joanne: (3) *My*/*I* name's Joanne. (4) Where are *your*/*you* from?
Kate: (5) *I'm*/*are* from Canada. And you?
Joanne: (6) *I'm*/*You* from Australia.

VOCABULARY

7 Countries
Find eight (8) countries in the box.
Look [→] and [↓].

```
B R I T A L S A M V U
A C O U M B W F I H A
G N X R T R H O P Y R
R G P C L I A P O L G
C T E I B T N C L A E
A U S T R A L I A S N
N R T A P I T A N E T
A K A L A N D U D B I
D E T Y I E B Q V Y N
P Y S E I R U S S I A
C A N A D A K U G M P
```

8 Cities
Write the letters in the correct order.

1 omeR   Rome
2 nnoLdo   ....
3 tAnseh   ....
4 wasWra   ....
5 eNw rokY   ....
6 sunBeo sieAr ....

9 I'm from ...
Complete the sentences. Write the names and the countries.

Poland, Britain (x2), Argentina, Italy, Greece

1 I'm Adam. I'm from *Poland*.

2 My name's .... I'm from ....

3 I'm .... I'm ....

4 My .... I ....

5 I .... I ....

6 My .... I ....

1 Hello

2 GRAMMAR
he/she/it is, Who? his/her/its

1 ★ **he/she is**
Write sentences about the nationalities.

1. Jamie/Britain *Jamie is British.*
2. Kostas/Greece ....
3. Paola/Italy ....
4. Gabriela/Argentina ....
5. Adam/Poland ....
6. Megan/Britain ....

2 ★ **Affirmative: Full and short forms**
Complete the sentences like the example.

Markos

1. Markos *is* Greek. *He's* from Athens.

Chiara

2. Chiara .... Italian. .... from Rome.

Arek

3. Arek .... Polish. .... from Warsaw.

Stacy

4. Stacy .... American. .... from New York.

Paul

5. Paul .... British. .... from London.

Cristina

6. Cristina .... Argentinian. .... from Buenos Aires.

3 ★ **Negative**
Write the sentences with short forms.

1. Kostas is Polish.
   Kostas isn't Polish.
2. Paola is from Warsaw.
   ....
3. My favourite pop star is American.
   ....
4. My penfriend is Italian.
   ....
5. My favourite sports star is Argentinian.
   ....
6. Megan is from London.
   ....

4 ★★ **Affirmative and negative**
Write pairs of sentences with short forms.

1. My favourite star/American (✗).
   She/Canadian (✓).
   My favourite star isn't American.
   She's Canadian.
2. My favourite music/heavy metal (✗).
   It/soul (✓).
   ....
   ....
3. My penfriend/from London (✗).
   He/from Cambridge (✓).
   ....
   ....
4. My penfriend/Russian (✗).
   She/Polish (✓).
   ....
   ....
5. My favourite sports star/from the USA (✗).
   He/from Brazil (✓).
   ....
   ....
6. My name/Kate (✗).
   It/Katie (✓).
   ....
   ....

Hello 1

5 ★★ Questions and short answers
Write questions and true answers.

1. your teacher/British
   Is your teacher British?
   Yes, he/she is./No, he/she isn't.
2. your favourite pop star/Italian
   .... ?
3. your favourite sports star/from Russia
   .... ?
4. your favourite music/heavy metal
   .... ?
5. your favourite film star/from the United States
   .... ?
6. your city/great?
   .... ?

6 ★ Who/What/Where questions
Complete the questions.

1. *What* 's your name?
2. .... are you from?
3. .... 's your favourite pop star?
4. .... 's your favourite film star?
5. .... 's your favourite music?
6. .... is your teacher from?

7 ★ he/his, she/her, it/its
Circle the correct word.

1. My penfriend is from Poland. (He's)/His great.
2. My teacher is British. Her/She name's Anna.
3. Gabriela is Argentinian. He's/She's from Rosario.
4. Kostas isn't Polish. She's/He's Greek.
5. My favourite music is heavy metal. It's/Its great!
6. My penfriend is from Italy. He's/His name is Marco.
7. Paola isn't from Spain. He's/She's from Italy.
8. I'm from a city in England. Its/It's name is Oxford.

8 ★★ I/she/he/it
In your notebook, write true answers to the questions in Exercise 6.

1 My name's ...

VOCABULARY

9 Countries and nationalities
Complete the table.

Use the Mini-dictionary to help you.

Country	Nationality
Britain	*British*
Greece	Greek
....	Polish
....	English
Spain	....
....	Italian
Argentina	....
Brazil	....
Russia	....
....	American
....	Canadian
France	....

10 Circle the correct word.

1. My penfriend is from French/(France).
2. Gabriela is in England/English.
3. My favourite star is from the United States/American.
4. Are you Argentinian/Argentina?
5. Is your teacher Poland/Polish?
6. Kostas is Greek/Greece.

1 Hello

Reading and Writing

1) True or false?
Read the e-mail. Are these sentences true (T) or false (F)?
Tick (✓) the correct box.

1 Teresa is from Sydney.
   T   F

2 Antonio Banderas is Spanish.
   T   F

3 Robbie Williams is Russian.
   T   F

4 Anna Kournikova is a pop star.
   T   F

To: kate williams
From: teresa davies
Subject: penfriends

Hi kate,

My names teresa davies. Im your new penfriend. Im from sydney in australia.

My favourite film star is from spain. His names antonio banderas and hes great! My favourite pop star is robbie williams. Hes english. My favourite sports star isnt english. Shes from Russia. Her names anna kournikova. My favourite music is soul.

Whats your favourite music? Whos your favourite star? Is he/she from australia?

Write soon.

teresa

2) Punctuation: Capital letters
Correct the e-mail in your notebook. Write the capital letters.

To: Kate Williams
From: Teresa Davies
Subject: Penfriends

Hi Kate,

3) Punctuation: Short forms
Correct the e-mail. Put '.

Hi Kate,

My name's Teresa Davies. I'm your new penfriend.

4) Spelling
Correct these spelling mistakes.

1 Inglish   *English*
2 Torkey   ....
3 polish   ....
4 Amerikan   ....
5 Espain   ....
6 Canadien   ....
7 Brasil   ....
8 Argentinan ....
9 Rusia   ....
10 Grece   ....

 Check your answers in the Mini-dictionary.

Hello 1

CHECK YOUR GRAMMAR AND VOCABULARY

1 *to be + I, you, he/she/it*
Circle the correct word. (0.5 marks each)

1 *I'm/are* Helen. *What's/What* your name?
2 You *is/are* from Cambridge and *she's/she* from London.
3 *Is/Am* he your penfriend? No, he *is/isn't*.
4 *Are/Is* New York great? Yes, it *is/it's*.
5 *Am/Are* you Polish? Yes, *I am/I'm*.

[5]

2 *What? Who? Where?*
Write questions for these answers. (1 mark each)

1 .... ?
My name's Andrew.
2 .... ?
I'm from New York.
3 .... ?
My favourite sports star is David Beckham.
4 .... ?
My favourite music is soul.
5 .... ?
My penfriend is from Poland.

[5]

3 *I/my, you/your, he/his, she/her, it/its*
Choose the correct form. (0.5 marks each)

1 *My/I'm* in London. *It's/Its* great.
2 *You/Your* penfriend is from Argentina. *She/Her* name's Julia.
3 *Her/She* favourite sports star is French. *He's/His* name's Fabien Barthez.
4 *He/His* favourite pop star is Britney Spears. *She's/Her* American.
5 *My/I* penfriend is from Brazil. *His/He's* great.

[5]

4 Countries and nationalities
Write the words in the correct list.
(0.5 marks each)

Brazil, Russian, Polish, Greece, American, Italy, Argentinian, British, Slovakia, England

Countries	Nationalities
....	....
....	....
....	....
....	....
....	....

[5]

Check your progress

Choose the correct answer. (1.5 marks each)

1 I .... from Warsaw.
   a) is   b) my   c) 'm   d) are
2 He .... from Athens.
   a) 's   b) are   c) not   d) am
3 You .... great!
   a) is   b) are   c) be   d) am
4 I .... Italian.
   a) no   b) 'm not   c) isn't   d) aren't
5 Hello. I'm your new teacher. .... name's Chris.
   a) My   b) I   c) He   d) Am
6 She .... from the United States.
   a) am   b) aren't   c) not   d) isn't
7 Is he Polish? No, he ....
   a) isn't   b) aren't   c) is   d) not
8 She's from Spain. .... name's Marta.
   a) She   b) His   c) She's   d) Her
9 Are you English? No, I ....
   a) aren't   b) 'm not   c) isn't   d) am
10 His name's Simon. .... 's my penfriend.
   a) He's   b) He   c) His   d) She

[15]

TOTAL: [35]

2 Meet the family

3 GRAMMAR

you/we/they are, How old? his/her, our, their

1 ★ you/we/they are
Write sentences with full forms.

1 They/from Cambridge
   They are from Cambridge.
2 We/Italian
   ....
3 You and your parents/from Wales
   ....
4 Gabriela and Paola/at home
   ....
5 Kostas and Adam/at school
   ....
6 The children/at the cinema
   ....

2 ★ you/we/they aren't
Write negative sentences with short forms.

1 They/at the cinema.
   They aren't at the cinema.
2 We/Polish
   ....
3 You and your family/from Italy
   ....
4 My brother and I/from London
   ....
5 My parents/Russian
   ....

3 ★★ Affirmative and negative
Write pairs of sentences with short forms.

1 They/from Poland (✗). They/from Slovakia (✓).
   They aren't from Poland. They're from Slovakia.
2 Mr and Mrs Williams/from England (✗). They/from Wales (✓).
   ....
3 We/from Buenos Aires (✗). We/from Rosario (✓).
   ....
4 Jamie and Megan/at home (✗). They/at the cinema (✓).
   ....
5 My sisters/at school (✗). They/at home (✓).
   ....
6 My brother and I/Argentinian (✗). We/Brazilian (✓).
   ....

4 ★★ Questions and short answers
Write the questions and true short answers.

1 your parents/at home
   Are your parents at home? Yes, they are./No, they aren't.
2 you and your friends/at school
   ....? ....
3 you and your family/Greek
   ....? ....
4 your friends/at the cinema
   ....? ....
5 your parents/from Poland
   ....? ....
6 your teachers/from England
   ....? ....

5 ★ we/our, you/your, they/their
Circle the correct word.

1 (They)/Their aren't at home now.
2 We/Our teacher is from Rome.
3 What are you/your names?
4 We/Our aren't from Warsaw.
5 Where are you/your from?
6 Their/They names are Simon and Claire.

Meet the family 2

6 ★★ How old?
Write questions and true answers.

1 How old/your penfriend
How old is your penfriend?
He's/She's (seventeen)

2 How old/you
....?
....

3 How old/your friend
....?
....

4 How old/parents
....?
....

7 ★★ to be; my, his/her, their
Complete the text.

(1) *My* name's Emily Walker. I (2) .... sixteen. My family and I (3) .... from Cambridge in England. My father (4) .... forty. (5) .... name's John. My mother (6) .... thirty-eight. (7) .... name's Anna. My grandparents (8) .... from London. (9) .... names are Alexander and Eve. What's your name? How old (10) .... you?

8 ★★★ to be; I/my, he/his, she/her
Look at the notes 1–5. Write sentences about you and your family in your notebook.

1 you – where from?/name?/how old?
2 you – where from?/name?/how old?
3 mother – where from?/name?/how old?
4 father – where from?/name?/how old?
5 brother/sister – where from?/name?/how old?

1 I'm from Brazil. My name's Silvia. I'm 17.

VOCABULARY

9 Families
Write the words in the correct list.

husband, wife, parents, sister, son, daughter, mother, grandfather, grandparents, grandmother, father, brother

husband	wife	parents
....	....	....
....	....	....
....	....	....
....	....	....

Check your answers in the Mini-dictionary.

10 Numbers
Match the numbers in the box and the words, like the example.

1   3   17   22   50   30   13
63   70   14   91   100

1 ☐ sixty-three   7 ☐ a/one hundred
2 ☐ fifty   8 [1] one
3 ☐ three   9 ☐ twenty-two
4 ☐ seventeen   10 ☐ fourteen
5 ☐ thirty   11 ☐ seventy
6 ☐ ninety-one   12 ☐ thirteen

11 Complete the crossword with the numbers in words.

Across
1 *7*
5 *9*
6 *18*
7 *80*
8 *40*
9 *15*

Down
2 *93*
3 *20*
4 *11*

2 Meet the family

4 GRAMMAR
a/an, possessive 's

1 ★ *a/an*
Write *a* or *an*.

1 *a* student
2 *an* engineer
3 ...... pop star
4 ...... actress
5 ...... teacher
6 ...... electrician
7 ...... scientist
8 ...... businesswoman

2 ★★ *a/an*
Write *a* or *an* in the correct place.

1 My parents are from Rome. My dad is *a* teacher.
2 My sister is student. She is at university in Istanbul.
3 My mother is actress. She's great!
4 Our brother is architect. His name's Andy.
5 Their daughter is engineer and their son is actor.
6 He isn't electrician. He's engineer.

3 ★ **Possessive 's**
Write *'s* in the correct place.

1 Chris is Mark*'s* brother.
2 You are my daughter teacher.
3 Nick is Angela father.
4 What is your mother name?
5 Linda favourite star is Johnny Depp.
6 What is your dad job?

4 ★★ *to be* or possessive *'s*?
Write *P* for possessive *'s* or write *is*.

1 She's a model. *is*
2 Dad's sister is a student. *P*
3 Jamie's favourite star is David Beckham. ....
4 Megan is Jamie's sister. ....
5 Jamie's at school. ....
6 What is your brother's name? ....
7 Who's your favourite star? ....
8 Adam's sixteen. ....

5 ★★ *to be* and possessive *'s*
Look at the family tree and write sentences.

1 Bill/Helen
   Bill is Helen's husband.
2 Greg and Adam/Kate
   Greg and Adam are Kate's brothers.
3 Kate/Helen
   ....
4 Greg and Adam/Helen
   ....
5 Kate/Adam
   ....
6 Bill and Helen/Greg
   ....

6 ★★ *a/an, to be,* possessive *'s*
Correct the mistakes.

1 ~~Shes~~ *she's* an engineer.
2 My ~~sisters~~ .... husband is a doctor.
3 ~~Where he~~ .... from?
4 ~~Mark~~ .... favourite pop group is ~~Westlife~~.
5 His mum is ~~a~~ .... architect.
6 Are you ~~an~~ .... student?

Meet the family 2

VOCABULARY

7 Jobs
Match the jobs with the pictures.

 Use the Mini-dictionary to help you.

businesswoman, teacher, architect, student, scientist, actor, engineer, secretary

1 *businesswoman* 2 .... 3 .... 4 ....

5 .... 6 .... 7 .... 8 ....

8 Write sentences about the people in Exercise 1 in your notebook.

1 She's a businesswoman.

9 Prepositions
Circle the correct word.

1 We're *at*/*from* Cambridge.
2 They aren't *from*/*at* the cinema.
3 My teacher is *at*/*from* school now.
4 Where are you *from*/*at*?
5 Is your sister *at*/*from* university?
6 Are your parents *from*/*at* home?
7 Are they *at*/*from* the United States?

Word Corner

1 Dictionary work
Look at your Mini-dictionary.

Write the correct picture page numbers.

1 Countries – pages ....
2 Families – page ....
3 Animals – pages ....
4 Jobs – page ....
5 The A–Z section is on pages ....

2 Spelling
Correct these spelling mistakes.

1 Briten   *Britain*
2 Italien   ....
3 dauhter   ....
4 fivety   ....
5 secretry   ....
6 arkitect   ....

Check your answers.

11

2 Meet the family

Reading and Writing

1) Punctuation: Capital letters and full stops
Read the text below. Put full stops (.) and capital letters where necessary.

My family by Emily Adams

our surname is Adams we are from Toronto in Canada my mums name is Sarah she is thirty-nine years old and she is an engineer mums favourite pop star is Elton John my dads name is Greg he is an electrician and he is forty-two his favourite film star is Sean Connery my sisters name is Linda and my brothers name is David Linda is fourteen and David is twelve Lindas favourite pop stars are The Backstreet Boys and Davids favourite is Will Smith my name is Emily I am seventeen and I am a student my favourite pop star is Britney Spears Britneys music is great!

2) Reading
Read the text again. Answer these questions.

1. Where is Emily from?
2. How old is she?
3. Who is Linda?
4. Who is David?
5. How old is Emily's mother?
6. What is Greg's job?

3) Punctuation: Apostrophes
Correct the text. Put apostrophes (') where necessary. Start like this.

My mum's name is Sarah.

4) Spelling
Correct these spelling mistakes.

1. sinema — *cinema*
2. eiht — ....
3. foto — ....
4. granmother — ....
5. intresting — ....
6. sientist — ....
7. univercity — ....
8. bussinesman — ....

Check your answers in the Mini-dictionary.

CHECK YOUR GRAMMAR AND VOCABULARY

Meet the family 2

1 we/you/they are
Complete the sentences. (0.5 mark each)

1 They .... from Barcelona in Spain.
2 .... you and your family Italian? No, we ....
3 We .... students.
4 .... they at home? Yes, they ....

[3]

2 Questions and answers
Correct the mistakes. (0.5 marks each)

1 How old ~~you are~~? ~~I~~ seventeen.
2 How old ~~are~~ your sister? ~~She~~ twenty.
3 What's ~~you~~ name? Are ~~your~~ American?
4 ~~They're~~ names are Chris and Sue. ~~Their~~ students.

[4]

3 a/an and possessive 's
Write 's in the correct place and a or an. (0.5 marks each)

1 My father name is Adam. He isn't .... engineer.
2 What is your penfriend name? Is she .... student?
3 Is your friend favourite star .... actor?
4 Is her sister husband .... sports star?

[4]

4 Family
Read the text. Write the names on the family tree. (1 mark each)

Tim's wife is Helen. Their son's name is Mark. Mark's sister is Rachel. James is Rachel's husband. Their son's name is Paul and their daughter's name is Claire.

Tim ... 1 ....
2 .... 3 .... 4 ....
Paul 5 ....

[5]

5 Numbers
Write the numbers as words. (0.5 marks each)

1 13 ....   5 15 ....
2 30 ....   6 50 ....
3 14 ....   7 19 ....
4 40 ....   8 90 ....

[4]

Check your progress

Complete the dialogue. (1 mark each)

Andy: Hello, I'm your new teacher.
Pedro: (1) .... your name?
Andy: My name's Andy.
Julia: (2) .... you English?
Andy: No, I (3) .... I'm from Perth. (4) .... 's a city in Australia. My wife (5) .... English.
Pedro: What's (6) .... name?
Andy: Fiona. She's (7) .... doctor. What (8) .... your names?
Pedro: My name's Pedro ...
Julia: And my name's Julia.
Andy: (9) .... are you from?
Julia: (10) .... 're from Rosario (11) .... Argentina.
Andy: And how old (12) .... you?
Pedro: I (13) .... fifteen and Julia (14) .... sixteen.
Julia: Pedro is (15) .... brother.

[15]

TOTAL: [35]

3 At home

5 GRAMMAR

have got, *the* and *a/an*

1 ★ **I/you/we/they/have got**
Write sentences with full forms.

1 I/a computer
   I have got a computer.
2 You/a camera
   ....
3 We/a garden
   ....
4 They/a dog
   ....
5 I/a cat
   ....
6 We/a CD player
   ....

2 ★ **Short forms**
Write the short forms for Exercise 1 in your notebook.

   1 I've got a computer.

3 ★ **I/you/we/they/haven't got**
Write these sentences in the negative with short forms.

1 I've got a sister.
   I haven't got a sister.
2 We've got a pet.
   ....
3 They've got a computer.
   ....
4 You've got a video.
   ....
5 I've got a TV.
   ....
6 They've got a garden.
   ....

4 ★★ **Questions and answers**
Write questions and true short answers.

1 you/a sister
   Have you got a sister? Yes, I have./No, I haven't.
2 your parents/a computer
   ....? ....
3 you/a dog
   ....? ....
4 you and your parents/a video
   ....? ....
5 your parents/a TV/in their bedroom
   ....? ....
6 you/a CD player/in your bedroom
   ....? ....

5 ★ ***a, an* or *the*?**
Circle the correct word.

1 We've got (**a**)/an cat and (**a**)/an dog. (**The**)/A/An cat's name is Felix.
2 I've got *a/an* old computer and *a/an* new CD player. *The/A/An* CD player is from Germany.
3 They've got *a/an* big house and *a/an* small garden. They are in *the/a/an* garden now.
4 I've got *a/an* boring game and *a/an* interesting game. *The/A/An* boring game is called Powertime.
5 We've got *a/an* computer and *a/an* video. *The/A/An* computer is new.

6 ★★ ***a, an* or *the*?**
Complete the text with *a*, *an* or *the*.

I've got (1) *an* English CD and (2) .... English video. (3) .... CD is boring, but (4) .... video is interesting. In my bedroom, I've got (5) .... computer and (6) .... CD player. (7) .... computer is big and (8) .... CD player is small.

14

At home 3

VOCABULARY

7 Homes
Match the numbers in the picture with the words.

bedroom	1	bath	
sofa		cooker	
toilet		bathroom	
sitting room		carpet	
kitchen		shower	
fridge		bed	
table		lamp	

 Check your answers in the Mini-dictionary.

8 Prepositions
Draw these objects in the house.

computer, CD player, TV, video

Now write four sentences in your notebook.

1 The (computer) is in the (bedroom).

9 Opposites
Write the opposites of these adjectives.

1. bad — *good*
2. .... — interesting
3. small — ....
4. .... — old

10 Adjectives
Write the adjectives in the correct place in the sentences. Change *a* to *an* where necessary.

1. I've got a video. (interesting)
   I've got an interesting video.
2. Have you got a computer? (new)
   ....
3. We've got a TV. (old)
   ....
4. Have they got a garden? (big)
   ....
5. Is she a teacher? (good)
   ....

11 Write the sentences in the plural.

1. My teacher is great.
   My teachers are great.
2. The room is small.
   ....
3. My book isn't boring.
   ....
4. Your sister is great.
   ....
5. Our friend is English.
   ....

3 At home

6 GRAMMAR
has got, have got/has got

1 ★ *he/she/it/has got*
Look at the pictures and write sentences.

1 Matthew has got a TV and he's got a computer.

2 Emma ....

3 Tim ....

4 Jane ....

5 Andy ....

2 ★ *he/she/it/hasn't got*
Write these sentences in the negative.

1 Our school has got a garden.
   Our school hasn't got a garden.
2 My brother has got a camera.
   ....
3 My grandfather has got a cat.
   ....
4 Our classroom has got a window.
   ....
5 Megan has got a sister.
   ....

3 ★★ **Affirmative and negative**
Look at the table. Complete the sentences about Mike and Jo with short forms.

	Mike	Jo	Peter	Tina
a brother	✗	✓	✓	✗
a sister	✓	✗	✓	✓
a penfriend	✓	✓	✗	✓
a cat	✓	✗	✓	✗
a dog	✗	✗	✗	✓

1 Mike *hasn't got* a brother, but *he's got* a sister.
2 Jo .... a brother, but she .... a sister.
3 Mike .... a penfriend and Jo .... a penfriend.
4 Mike .... a cat, but he .... a dog.
5 Jo .... a pet.

4 ★★ **Questions and answers**
Look at the table in Exercise 3. Write questions and short answers about Peter and Tina in your notebook.

1 Peter/a brother
2 Tina/a cat
3 Peter/a sister
4 Tina/a penfriend
5 Peter/a dog
6 Tina/a sister

1 Has Peter got a brother? Yes, he has.
2 Has Tina got a cat? No, she hasn't.

16

At home 3

5 ★★★ **have/has got**
Complete the dialogue with the correct form.

Helen: Hello.
Diane: Hi, Helen. Are you in your new house now?
Helen: Yes, it's great!
I (1) *'ve got* a big bedroom and the house (2) .... a nice garden.
Diane: What (3) .... you .... in your bedroom?
Helen: I (4) .... a new computer and a CD player. My brother (5) .... a TV in his room.
Diane: (6) .... he .... a video, too?
Helen: No, he (7) .... It's in the sitting room.
Diane: (8) .... you .... pets in the new house?
Helen: Yes, we (9) .... two small white cats. They're in the garden now.
Diane: Great!

VOCABULARY

6 Colours
Write the letters in the correct order.

1 erd — *red*
2 elbu — ....
3 klbca — ....
4 kinp — ....
5 oelylw — ....
6 thiwe — ....
7 enroga — ....
8 ergen — ....

What are your favourite colours? Number the colours. (1 = favourite).

7 Complete the sentences.

1 Red + ... = pink
2 White + ... = grey
3 .... + ... = green
4 .... + ... = orange

8 **My room**
Find the names of the objects (1–7). Write them on the picture.

Use the Mini-dictionary to help you.

9 Look at the picture of the bedroom. Read and complete the text.

My name's Angela. I'm seventeen. I've got a new (1) *bedroom* . It's great! It's got a big (2) .... and two (3) .... of my favourite stars on the (4) .... I've got a new (5) .... for my computer and two (6) .... I've got (7) .... for my books and a (8) .... for my favourite music, but I haven't got a TV or a video.

10 Write about your bedroom in your notebook. Use these ideas.

> my room/(green) walls – it/a (yellow) carpet
> – it/a (big) window
> I/a TV – I/a video – I/CD player
>
> My room has got green walls.

3 At home

Reading and Writing

1) Reading
Read the text, *My house*. Complete the table.

Has Todd got	Yes (✓)	No (✗)
a garden?	✓	
a pet?		
a green carpet?		
a computer?		
shelves?		
posters?		

My house

My name's Todd and my surname is French. I'm from the United States. My family and I have got a house in Texas. The house has got five bedrooms two bathrooms a big kitchen and a sitting room. It's got white walls big windows and a great garden.

My room is nice. It's got green walls a blue carpet and red chairs. I've got a small computer and a CD player, but I haven't got a TV in my bedroom. Our TV is in the sitting room. I've got big shelves for my books CDs and computer games.

2) Read the text again and circle the correct information.

1. Todd is *American/French*.
2. Todd's house has got *eight/nine* rooms.
3. The house has got a big *sitting room/kitchen*.
4. The walls in Todd's bedroom are *green/blue*.

3) Punctuation: Commas
Correct the text. Put commas (,) where necessary.

The house has got five bedrooms, two bathrooms, a big kitchen and a sitting room.

4) Put commas (,) where necessary in these sentences.

1. Our school has got a computer a CD player and a video.
2. My favourite colours are red blue green and pink.
3. I've got a brother a sister and a penfriend.
4. The TV video CD player lamp and piano are in the sitting room.
5. Their friends are from London New York Rome Athens and Warsaw.

5) Spelling
Correct these spelling mistakes.

1. camara — *camera*
2. frige — ....
3. clasroom — ....
4. yelow — ....
5. borring — ....
6. oranje — ....
7. fone — ....
8. toillet — ....

Check your answers in the Mini-dictionary.

Word Corner

Find the words in your Mini-dictionary. Use the A–Z Section.

1. dog — *page 40*
2. the United States — ....
3. Spanish — ....
4. computer programmer — ....
5. grandmother — ....
6. thirty — ....
7. bathroom — ....
8. shower — ....

At home 3

CHECK YOUR GRAMMAR AND VOCABULARY

1 have/has got, haven't/hasn't got
Complete the sentences with the correct form. (0.5 marks each)

1 I .... two penfriends. They're British.
2 She .... a TV. It's in her bedroom.
3 .... you .... a pet? No, I ....
4 We've got a dog, but we .... a cat.
5 .... he .... a big house?
   Yes, he ....
6 They .... a new computer game.
7 He's got a brother, but he .... a sister.
8 My room is great! It .... blue walls and a red carpet.

[5]

2 a/an/the
Complete the sentences with *a*, *an* or *the*. (0.5 marks each)

1 I've got .... garden. My pets are in .... garden now.
2 They've got .... new house, but they aren't in .... house now.
3 We've got .... English teacher and .... art teacher. .... English teacher is new.
4 She's got .... letter and .... e-mail. .... e-mail is from her penfriend.

[5]

3 Homes
Match the objects (1–8) with the rooms (a–d). (0.5 marks each)

1 toilet   a) bedroom
2 fridge   b) kitchen
3 cooker   c) sitting room
4 video   d) bathroom
5 bath
6 bed
7 shower
8 sofa

[4]

4 Adjectives and colours
Write the words in the correct list. (0.5 marks each)

good, green, white, bad, black, boring, nice, grey, interesting, pink, small, yellow

Adjectives   Colours
....
....
....
....
....
....

[6]

Check your progress

Circle the correct word. (1 mark each)

Karen: Hello. What's your name?
Isabel: Isabel. I'm (1) *at/from* Italy.
Karen: (2) *My/I* name's Karen. Welcome to England. (3) *Are/Am* your parents in England?
Isabel: No, they (4) *isn't/aren't*. They're (5) *at/from* home in Italy. We (6) *'ve got/'s got* a house in Rome.
Karen: (7) *Has/Have* you got a garden?
Isabel: Yes, we have. And I've got (8) *a/an* big bedroom. (9) *He's/It's* got white walls, big windows and a nice, red carpet.
Karen: I've got a new CD player (10) *at/in* my bedroom. And my brother (11) *have/has* got a new TV!
Isabel: (12) *What/How* old is your brother?
Karen: He (13) *has/is* 21. (14) *Her/His* name's David and he's (15) *a/the* student.

[15]

TOTAL: [35]

4 At school

7 GRAMMAR
this and *that*

1 ★ *this* or *that*?
Write *this* or *that* with the pictures.

 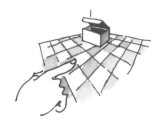

1 *this* book   2 .... box

3 .... bag   4 .... clock

2 ★ *this/that* + nouns
Complete the sentences.

3 ★★ *What's this/that?*
Write questions and answers.

1 Q: *What's this* ?
   A: *It's a book.*

2 Q: *What's that* ?
   A: *It's a computer.*

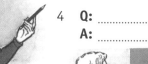

3 Q: .... ?
   A: ....

4 Q: .... ?
   A: ....

5 Q: .... ?
   A: ....

Pass me *that book* , please.

Come here. Look at .... on the wall.

Give me .... , please.

What's in .... here?

At school 4

VOCABULARY

/eɪ/	/iː/	/e/	/aɪ/	/əʊ/	/uː/	/ɑː/
a	b	f	i	o	q	r

4 The alphabet
Write the letters in the correct part of the table.

a b c d e f g h i
j k l m n o p q r
s t u v w x y z

5 The classroom
Write the names of the objects (1–12) in the picture.

 Check your answers in the Mini-dictionary.

6 Where are they?
Write sentences with *on*. Look at the things in the picture.

1 box
   The box is on the shelf.
2 clock and poster
   ....
3 bag
   ....
4 pens
   ....

7 Lessons and objects
Match the objects (a–h) with the lessons (1–8).

1 [f] English
2 [ ] art
3 [ ] computer studies
4 [ ] maths
5 [ ] literature
6 [ ] music
7 [ ] sport
8 [ ] geography

8 In your notebook, write the names of the objects in Exercise 7.

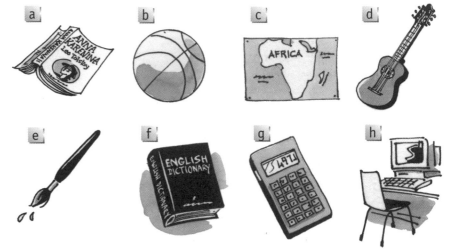

a) book

Check your answers in the Mini-dictionary.

4 At school

8 GRAMMAR
Plural nouns, *these* and *those*

1 ★ **Plural nouns**
Write the plurals.

1 pencil pencils
2 poster ....
3 magazine ....
4 dictionary ....
5 shelf ....
6 box ....
7 family ....
8 watch ....
9 student ....
10 actress ....
11 wife ....
12 city ....

2 ★ ***these* or *those*?**
Write *these* or *those* with the pictures.

1 *these* books   2 .... posters

3 .... graphs   4 .... videos

3 ★ ***these/those* + nouns**
Complete the sentences.

4 ★★ ***What are these/those*?**
Write questions and answers.

1 Q: *What are these* ?
  A: *They're magazines.*

2 Q: *What are those* ?
  A: *They're boxes.*

3 Q: .... ?
  A: ....

4 Q: .... ?
  A: ....

5 Q: .... ?
  A: ....

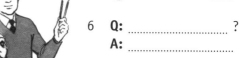

6 Q: .... ?
  A: ....

1 Look at *these magazines*. They're great.
2 .... are boring.
3 Pass me .... , please.
4 .... are really nice!

5 ★★ to be, these/those + plural nouns
Write these sentences in the plural.

1 This book is interesting.
   These books are interesting.
2 That poster is great!
   ....
3 What's this? It's a magazine.
   ....
4 What's that? It's a graph.
   ....
5 Look at this dictionary.
   ....
6 Pass me that box, please.
   ....

VOCABULARY

6 Objects
Write the words in the correct part of the diagram.

pencil, encyclopedia, pen, camera, watch, piece of paper, newspaper, rubber, magazine, clock

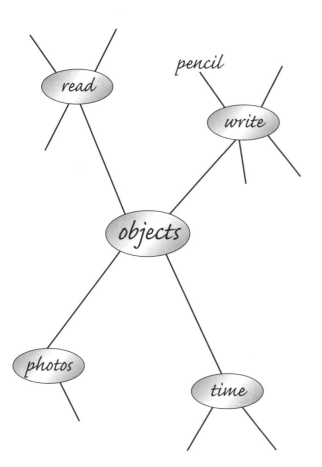

7 Answer the questions with true answers in your notebook.

1 What have you got in your bag?
2 What have you got in your classroom?
3 What have you got on your desk?
4 What have your got on the wall?

1 I've got a pen in my bag.

8 Questions and answers
Match the questions (1–4) with the answers (a–d).

1 How do you spell 'pencil'?   [b]
2 What's this in English?   [ ]
3 Who is in that photo?   [ ]
4 What are those on your desk?   [ ]

a) It's Linda, my sister.
b) P – E – N – C – I – L.
c) They're maps of London.
d) It's a calculator.

Word Corner

Write these words in alphabetical order.

actor, piano, yellow, friend, read, carpet, pink, white, television, green, interesting, you, old

actor ....
....
....
....

Check your answers in the Mini-dictionary.

4 At school

Reading and Writing

1 Reading
Read the text. Match the text with the correct plan.

> **My timetable – Alison Ellis**
> My name is alison ellis. this is my school Its called St. peter's School. we've got six classrooms a computer room and a gym The classrooms are big, but the gym is small. we havent got an art room or a music room
>
> My classroom is number 6 Its got a board two cupboards shelves and posters on the wall Today is friday Ive got five lessons – maths science history art and computer studies. Maths science and history are boring, but art and computer studies are great! my favourite teachers name is mr williams. hes our art teacher. hes really interesting

PLAN A

classroom 1	classroom 2	classroom 3	art room
classroom 4	classroom 5	classroom 6	music room

PLAN B

classroom 1	gym	classroom 2	classroom 3
classroom 4	computer room	classroom 5	classroom 6

2 Read the text again. Are these sentences true (T) or false (F)?

1. Alison's school has got nine rooms. ☐
2. Alison's classroom is number six. ☐
3. Alison's classroom hasn't got a clock. ☐
4. The art teacher is boring. ☐

3 Punctuation

1. Correct the text. Write capital letters and full stops (.) where necessary.
2. Write commas (,) where necessary.
3. Write apostrophes (') and possessive 's where necessary.

> My name is Alison Ellis.
> This is my school.
> It's called St. Peter's School.
> We've got six classrooms, a computer room and a gym.

4 Spelling
Correct the spelling mistakes.

1. therty   _thirty_
2. repeet   ....
3. grean   ....
4. sirname ....
5. lern   ....
6. peeple   ....

5 Write the words in Exercise 4 in the correct list.

/ɜː/	/iː/
th**ir**ty	rep**ea**t
....	....
....	....

CHECK YOUR GRAMMAR AND VOCABULARY

1 *this/that, these/those*
Circle the correct word. (0.5 marks each)

1 Look at *this/these* magazine. It's great!
2 Come to the window! What's *that/this* in the street?
3 What are *that/those*? They're English cassettes.
4 *These/This* videos are boring!
5 Pass me *these/those* pens, please. They're on the desk.
6 The children are in the house. Who's *that/this* in the garden?

☐ 3

2 Plural nouns
Write the plurals. (0.5 marks each)

1 ruler ....
2 ball ....
3 shelf ....
4 city ....
5 wife ....
6 family ....
7 actress ....
8 box ....
9 watch ....
10 paintbrush ....

☐ 5

3 Lessons
Write the letters in the correct order. Start with the underlined letter. (0.5 marks)

1 tueoprcm sde<u>s</u>uit ....
2 cus<u>m</u>i ....
3 th<u>y</u>sior ....
4 r<u>s</u>otp ....
5 sln<u>e</u>ihg ....
6 reair<u>l</u>tetu ....

☐ 3

4 Classroom objects
Complete the crossword with the names of the objects. (1 mark each)

Across

Down

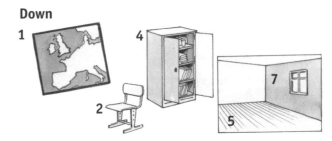

☐ 9

Check your progress

Choose the correct form. (1 mark each)

Ann: Come here, Sue. Look at (1) *this/these* photos of my new school!
Sue: OK. (2) *Who's/What's* that in the classroom?
Ann: That's my teacher, Mrs Reeves. (3) *He's/She's* great!
Sue: And where (4) *is/are* you in this photo?
Ann: I'm (5) *at/in* the art room. My picture is (6) *on/in* the wall.
Sue: (7) *It's/Its* great. The colours (8) *is/are* really nice.
Ann: Thank you. (9) *These/That* photos are of the computer room.
Sue: Look at the computers! (10) *They're/Their* great!
Ann: Yes. (11) *Have/Has* your school got (12) *the/a* computer room?
Sue: No, but I've got (13) *a/an* new computer (14) *in/at* home. Computer studies is my favourite lesson. What's (15) *your/you're* favourite lesson?
Ann: I've got two. Art and literature.

☐ 15

TOTAL: ☐ 35

5 Going out

9 GRAMMAR
Imperatives

1 ★ Affirmative

Write the words in the correct order. Write capital letters and full stops where necessary.

1 on/open/your/page/books/fifteen
   Open your books on page fifteen.
2 books/the/put/shelves/the/on
   ....
3 board/on/the/write/answer/the
   ....
4 bag/in/your/put/calculator/your
   ....
5 on/poster/at/look/the/wall/the
   ....
6 eight/on/the/read/text/page
   ....

2 ★ Negative

Write negative instructions.

1 go/to the disco
   Don't go to the disco.
2 open/that box
   Don't open that box
3 sit down/on this chair
   Don't sit down on this chair
4 put/your bags/on the bed
   Don't put your bags on the bed
5 buy/coffee/at that café
   Don't buy coffee at that café
6 write/on the board
   Don't write the board

3 ★★ Affirmative and negative

Match the instructions with the pictures.

Go to the gym.   Take an umbrella.   Sit down.
Don't touch the paintings.   Don't talk in the exam.
Don't be late.   Don't listen to music in class.
Open the window.

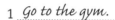

1 *Go to the gym.*   2 ....

3 ....   4 ....

5 ....   6 ....

7 ....   8 ....

Going out 5

4 ★★ Affirmative and negative
Write sentences.

1 café/great sandwiches
Go to that café. It's got great sandwiches.
2 bookshop/boring books
Don't go to that bookshop. It's got boring books.
3 disco/great music
Go to that disco. It's got great music.
4 restaurant/terrible food
Don't go to that restaurant. It's terrible food.
5 museum/interesting paintings
Go to that museum. It's got interesting paintings.
6 shop/expensive CDs
Don't go to that shop. It's got expensive CDs.

VOCABULARY

5 Places
Label the picture with the words.

disco, museum, café, church, street, cinema, mosque, hotel, main square, market, shop, restaurant, park, railway station

6 Write true sentences about the picture with *near*.

1 the cinema/the disco
The cinema is near the disco.
2 the shops/the market
The shops aren't near the market.
3 the restaurant/the railway station
The restaurant is near the railway station.
4 the café and the mosque/the park
The café and the mosque are near the park.
5 the museum/the church
The museum is near the church.
6 the disco and the cinema/the main square
The disco

7 Opposites
Write the opposites of these adjectives.

1 good *bad*
2 interesting boring
3 Fantastic terrible
4 cheap expensive
5 new ......
6 ...... big

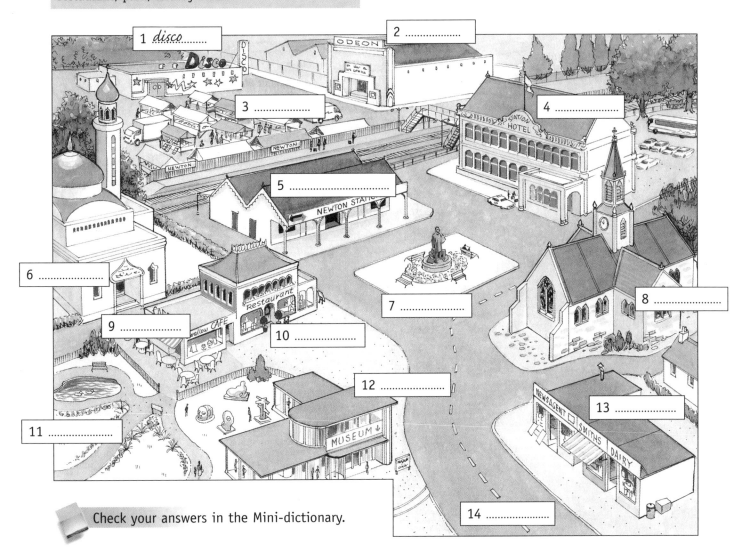

Check your answers in the Mini-dictionary.

5 Going out

10 GRAMMAR
some and any

1 ★ **some** (affirmative)
Write sentences.

1 I/CDs
   I've got some CDs.
2 My city/new shops
   My city has got new shops
3 We/coffee
   We have got some coffee
4 She/new T-shirts
   She has got new T-shirts
5 My friends/orange juice
   My friends have got some orange juice

2 ★ **any** (negative)
Write sentences.

1 I/not/stamps
   I haven't got any stamps.
2 You/not/paper
   ....
3 He/not/pens
   ....
4 My city/not/museums
   ....
5 We/not/tea
   ....

3 ★ **any** (questions)
Write questions and short answers.

1 you/pencils?
   Have you got any pencils?
   Yes, *I have*.
2 he/stamps?
   Has he got any stamps?
   No, *he hasn't*.
3 we/orange juice?
   Have we got orange juice?
   Yes, *we have*.
4 this city/parks?
   Has this city got any parks?
   Yes, *it has*.
5 your sister/CDs
   Has your sister got any CDs?
   No, *she hasn't*.

4 ★★ **some/any** (affirmative, negative and questions)
Complete the sentences with *some* or *any*.

1 We've got *some* stamps.
2 You haven't got *any* envelopes.
3 Have we got *any* mineral water?
4 She's got *some* cheese sandwiches.
5 We haven't got *any* coffee.
6 Have you got *any* postcards?

5 ★★ **some/any** (affirmative and negative)
Look at the shopping list. Write sentences.

- orange juice ✓
- mineral water ✗
- tea ✓
- coffee ✗
- envelopes ✓
- stamps ✗
- cheese ✓
- eggs ✗
- salad ✓
- tomatoes ✗

1 We've got some orange juice, but we haven't got any mineral water.
2 *We've got some tea, but we haven't got any coffee.*
3 *We've got some envelopes, but we haven't got any stamps.*
4 *We've got some cheese, but we haven't got any eggs.*
5 *We've got some salad, but we haven't got any tomatoes.*

6 ★★ **some/any** (affirmative and negative)
Write true sentences.

1 stamps in my bag
   *I've got some stamps in my bag./
   I haven't got any stamps in my bag.*
2 soul CDs
   ....
3 heavy metal CDs
   ....
4 posters in my room
   ....
5 new T-shirts
   ....
6 English books
   ....

28

Going out 5

7 ★★★ some/any
Think about your town or city. Write the dialogues in your notebook with true answers.

> **Tourist:** Has this town got any interesting museums?
> **You:** Yes, it has. The City Museum is near the main square. It's got some interesting paintings.

1 this town/interesting museums?
2 this town/interesting church?
3 this town/good discos?
4 this town/cheap shops?
5 this town/good cafés?

VOCABULARY

8 Food and drinks
Write the words in the correct list.

sandwich, orange juice, egg, salad, mineral water, tomato, coffee, cheese, tea

Food	Drinks
sandwich	_orange juice_
....	....
....	....
....	....
....	

9 Shopping
Write the names of the objects. Match the objects (1–8) with the shops (a–e).

10
Match the sentences (1–4) with (a–d) to make dialogues.

1 Go to the market. It's got some good CDs. [d]
2 A salad sandwich, please. [ ]
3 Four postcards of Cambridge, please. [ ]
4 Have you got any big football shirts? [ ]

a) Here you are.
b) I'm sorry. We haven't got any salad sandwiches.
c) Large or extra large?
d) That's interesting.

11
In your notebook, write a list of shops near your house.

Word Corner

Look at your Mini-dictionary.

1 Add two more shops to the list in Exercise 9.

   ....

2 Now find three places where you eat food and have a drink.

   ....

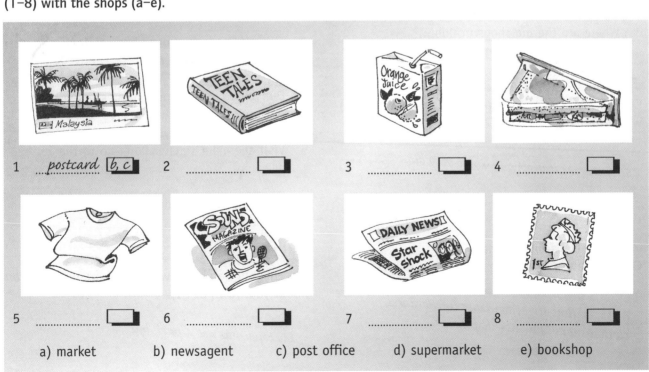

1 _postcard_ [b, c]   2 ....   3 ....   4 ....

5 ....   6 ....   7 ....   8 ....

a) market   b) newsagent   c) post office   d) supermarket   e) bookshop

5 Going out

Reading and Writing

1 Reading
Read the text. Match the photos with paragraphs 1, 2 and 3.

My City by Danny Carson

1 I am from Dublin in Ireland. it is the capital city it is not very big. It is beautiful. It is historic and interesting. visit Trinity College It has got some very old books
2 Dublin has got some great shops. go to Grafton street for department stores clothes shops and shoe shops. These shops are good. they are expensive. go to the markets for cheap clothes shoes and CDs
3 my favourite area is called Temple Bar. It has got cafés restaurants a cinema and a theatre. It is fantastic
4 The area near my house has got some shops it hasn't got any banks

2 Read the text again. Answer these questions.
1 Is Danny English?
2 Is Dublin an old city?
3 Where are the big shops in Dublin?
4 What has Temple Bar got?

3 Punctuation: Capital letters and full stops
Correct the text. Put capital letters and full stops (.) where necessary.

It is the capital city. It is not very big.

4 Punctuation: Commas
Correct the text. Put commas (,) where necessary.

Go to Grafton Street for department stores, clothes shops and shoe shops.

5 Linking with *but*
Look at these sentences. Link them with *but*. Change the capital letters where necessary.

1 It is not very big. It is beautiful.
   It is not very big but it is beautiful.
2 These shops are good. They are expensive.
   ....
3 The area near my house has got some shops. It hasn't got any banks.
   ....
4 Our town has got some interesting statues. It hasn't got any museums.
   ....
5 Visit the main square. Don't go to the museums.
   ....
6 This area has got some cafés. It hasn't got any restaurants.
   ....

6 In your notebook, write five sentences with *but* about your town or city.

My town has got a park but ...

Going out 5

CHECK YOUR GRAMMAR AND VOCABULARY

1 Imperatives
Complete the sentences with the correct form of the verbs in the box. (1 mark each)

drink, be, visit, talk, buy, go

1 .... the museum. It's very interesting.
2 .... the coffee. It's terrible.
3 Dinner is at 7.00. .... late.
4 .... to that clothes shop. It's got great T-shirts.
5 This is a test. .... to other students.
6 .... CDs at the market. They're very cheap.

[6]

2 some/any
Complete the sentences with *some* or *any*. (0.5 marks each)

1 I've got .... new CDs.
2 Have you got .... envelopes?
3 She hasn't got .... brothers or sisters.
4 The newsagent has got .... interesting magazines.
5 Have they got .... orange juice?
6 The shop hasn't got .... mineral water.
7 The shops have got .... nice postcards.
8 Has this café got .... sandwiches?

[4]

3 Places and objects
Match the objects with the places. (1 mark each)

1 food   a) cinema
2 T-shirt   b) disco
3 film   c) newsagent
4 magazine   d) café
5 football shirt   e) clothes shop
6 music   f) sports shop

[6]

4 Adjectives
Choose the correct word. (0.5 marks each)

1 That shop isn't *cheap/new*. It's very expensive.
2 Watch this video. It's really *good/bad*.
3 Don't go to that restaurant. The food is *fantastic/terrible*.
4 The town isn't boring. It's very *interesting/small*.

[2]

5 Food and drink
Write the words with the pictures. (0.5 marks each)

mineral water, sandwich, tomato, cheese

1 ....

2 ....

3 ....

4 ....

[2]

Check your progress

Circle the correct word. (1 mark each)

My town isn't very big but (1) *its/it's* very interesting. The centre and the main square (2) *is/are* old and very beautiful. The main square (3) *have/has* got a church and (4) *a/an* statue. The statue is of a famous doctor from (5) *our/we* city.

We (6) *have/has* got three museums, two theatres and five cinemas. (7) *You visit/Visit* the City Museum. It's got (8) *some/any* fantastic paintings and statues. The Modern Art Museum is (9) *at/near* the main square. (10) *This/These* museum is very interesting, (11) *and/but* very expensive, too.

My local area has got a market, three small shops and a bank. It hasn't got (12) *some/any* big shops or department stores. (13) *That/These* shops are in (14) *a/the* centre. Has your city got (15) *some/any* interesting places?

[15]

TOTAL: [35]

6 Playing sport

11 GRAMMAR
can and *can't*

1 ★ *can*
Write sentences.

1 I/play basketball
   I can play basketball.
2 He/play football
   ....
3 Gabriela/speak English
   ....
4 We/dive
   ....

2 ★ *can't*
Write negative sentences.

1 I/not/dive
   I can't dive.
2 You/not/play basketball
   ....
3 She/not/speak Spanish
   ....
4 My friends/not swim
   ....

3 ★ *can/can't*
Look at the table and write sentences.

1 Nicola/ski and do the high jump
   Nicola can ski and do the high jump.
2 Nicola and Simon/play tennis
   ....
   ....
3 Andy and Teresa/swim
   ....
4 Simon/ski and swim
   ....
   ....
5 Andy and Simon/do the high jump
   ....
   ....

4 ★★ *can/can't* in questions and answers
Look at the table in Exercise 3. Write questions and short answers.

1 Simon/ski
   Can Simon ski? Yes, he can.
2 Nicola/swim
   Can Nicola swim? No, ...
3 Nicola and Teresa/do the high jump
   ....? ....
4 Simon/swim?
   ....? ....
5 Nicola and Simon/play tennis?
   ....? ....

5 ★★ *can/can't* in questions and answers
Look at the table in Exercise 3. Write questions with question words and answers.

1 Who/play tennis
   Who can play tennis? Andy and Teresa can.
2 What sports/Andy do
   What sports can Andy do? ....
3 Who/do the high jump
   ....? ....
4 What sports/Simon do
   ....? ....
5 Who/do all four sports
   ....? ....

		🎿	🏊	🎾	🏃
Nicola		✓	✗	✗	✓
Andy		✗	✓	✓	✗
Teresa		✓	✓	✓	✓
Simon		✓	✓	✗	✗

Playing sport 6

6 ★★ can/can't
Write questions and true short answers in your notebooks.

1 you/ski

> 1 Can you ski?
> Yes, I can./No, I can't.

2 your mother/speak French?
3 your friend/play tennis?
4 you/speak Spanish?
5 your father/play football?
6 you and your friend/dive?

VOCABULARY

7 Sports
Write the words in the correct list.

the long jump, tennis, athletics, handball, fast, three metres, football, the 1,000 metres, basketball, the high jump, hockey, gymnastics, volleyball

play	do
tennis	
	run
jump	

9 Adverbs
Look at the table and complete the sentences.

Team	run	play basketball	swim	play football
France	(fast)	50	50	100
Britain	(fast)	25	50	75
Canada	(not fast)	75	50	25
Australia	(not fast)	75	100	25
USA	(not fast)	100	100	25

= fast   = not fast   25 = not very well
50 = well   75 = very well   100 = brilliantly

1 The Canadian and the American teams _can_ run _fast_ .
2 The American team _can't_ play football _very well_ .
3 The French team .... play football ....
4 The British team .... swim ....
5 The Australian and Canadian teams .... play basketball ....
6 The American team .... play basketball ....
7 The British, French and Australian teams .... run ....
8 The British team .... football ....

10
Write true sentences in your notebook. Use these ideas with can/can't and the adverbs in Exercise 9.

> I / Our basketball team / My friends / Our football team / My favourite sports star
> I can swim very well. / I can't swim very well.

8 Complete the sports crossword with the names of the sports.

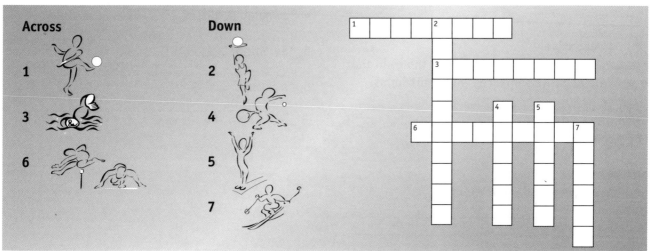

Across: 1, 3, 6
Down: 2, 4, 5, 7

6 Playing sport

12 GRAMMAR
there is/there are and there isn't/there aren't

1 ★ Affirmative
Look at the list and write sentences with full forms.

City Sports Centre
- gym
- 2 swimming pools
- café
- 6 tennis courts
- football pitch
- tennis classes
- aerobics classes
- shop

1 There is a gym.
2 There are two swimming pools.
3 ....
4 ....
5 ....
6 ....
7 ....
8 ....

2 ★ Affirmative
Look at Exercise 1. Write the sentences with the short forms of *there is* in your notebook.

1 There's a gym.

3 ★ Negative
The City Sports Centre hasn't got the things in the box. Write negative sentences with short forms.

jacuzzi, basketball courts, sauna, swimming classes, children's pool, indoor tennis courts, restaurant, diving classes

1 There isn't a jacuzzi.
2 There aren't basketball courts.
3 ....
4 ....
5 ....
6 ....
7 ....
8 ....

4 ★★ Affirmative and negative
Write sentences with short forms.

1 a café (✓) a restaurant (✗)
   There's a café but there isn't a restaurant.
2 tennis courts (✓) basketball courts (✗)
   There are tennis courts but there aren't basketball courts.
3 a jacuzzi (✓) a sauna (✗)
   ....
4 a football pitch (✓) football classes (✗)
   ....
5 a gym (✓) aerobics classes (✗)
   ....
   ....
6 two swimming pools (✓) a children's pool (✗)
   ....
   ....

5 ★★ Questions and short answers
Look at Exercise 1. Write questions and short answers about the City Sports Centre.

1 a gym
   Is there a gym? Yes, there is.
2 tennis courts
   Are there tennis courts? Yes, there are.
3 a restaurant
   ....
4 swimming classes
   ....
5 aerobics classes
   ....
6 a jacuzzi
   ....

Playing sport 6

6 ★★★ *there is/there are, have/has got, can/can't*
Complete the dialogue with the words in the box.

Is, can, has got (x2), are, can't, have got, Are

Tom: (1) ..*Is*.. there a sports centre near here?
Andy: Yes, there's a new place in Cambridge Street. It (2) ………… a fantastic pool.
Tom: But I (3) ………… swim.
Andy: Don't worry. There (4) ………… swimming classes and the sports centre (5) ………… a small pool for beginners.
Tom: Great! (6) ………… there tennis courts? I'm good at tennis and I (7) ………… a new racket.
Andy: I (8) ………… play tennis, too!
Tom: Good. Come to the sports centre with me!

VOCABULARY

7 Word pairs
Match the words (1–6) with (a–f).

1 swimming   a) courts
2 sports   b) pitch
3 football   c) centre
4 tennis   d) pool
5 aerobics   e) courts
6 basketball   f) classes

8 Write six sentences about your town/city in your notebooks. Use the words in Exercise 1 and *there is/there are, there isn't/there aren't*.

There is one swimming pool.

9 Times
Match the times in numbers (1–6) with the times in words (a–f).

1 4.15 p.m.   a) six o'clock in the evening
2 6.00 p.m.   b) seven forty-five in the evening
3 7.30 a.m.   c) two thirty in the afternoon
4 2.30 p.m.   d) six o'clock in the morning
5 7.45 p.m.   e) four fifteen in the afternoon
6 6.00 a.m.   f) seven thirty in the morning

10 Write the times.

1 2:05   It's two oh five.
2 8:15   …………………………………
3 4:00   …………………………………
4 10:25 …………………………………
5 11:45 …………………………………
6 1:30   …………………………………
7 3:55   …………………………………
8 9:20   …………………………………

11 Prepositions
Complete the sentences with *at* or *in*.

1 Dinner is ..*at*.. seven o'clock.
2 My aerobics class is …… the morning.
3 Maths is …… ten fifteen.
4 Art is …… the afternoon.
5 The sports centre is open …… 9.30 a.m.
6 Our tennis class is …… the evening.

12 Write five sentences about your lessons and classes in your notebook. Use *at* and *in*.

Word Corner

1 Write three words in each list.

Furniture at home:
sofa, …………… , …………… , ……………

Classroom objects:
board, …………… , …………… , ……………

Places in town:
museum, …………… , …………… , ……………

Check your answers in the Mini-dictionary.

2 Now write true sentences about these things in your notebook. Use *there is/there are*.

There's a big sofa in my sitting room.

6 Playing sport

Reading and Writing

1) Reading
Read the text and complete the form.

I'm Miss Ellen Howard. I'm eighteen and I'm from Montreal in Canada. I'm a student in Cambridge. My interests are art, history and sports. I can swim well and I can run fast. I can't play tennis very well, but I've got a good racket. My tennis classes at the Play Well Sports Centre are at 9.00 a.m. and 3.30 p.m. My teacher's name is Mr Cooper. He can play tennis brilliantly! I can speak English and French. I can speak Italian, too, but not very well.

Play Well Sports Centre

- Surname: (1) Howard
- First name: (2) ....
- Title: (3) .... Age: (4) ....
- Nationality: (5) ....
- Home town: (6) ....
- Occupation: (7) ....
- Interests: (8) ....
- Sports: (9) ....
- Class: (10) ....
- Time of classes: (11) ....
- Name of teacher: (12) ....

2) Read the text again. Are these sentences true (T) or false (F)?

1. Ellen is good at swimming. ☐
2. Ellen's racket isn't very good. ☐
3. Ellen's classes are in the morning and in the afternoon. ☐
4. Ellen can't speak French very well. ☐
5. Ellen is very good at Italian. ☐

3) Writing names and titles
Correct these names and titles. Put capital letters and full stops (.) where necessary.

1. miss e howard – Miss E. Howard
2. mr pj green – ....
3. mrs fr davies – ....
4. ms sl allen – ....
5. mr br ellis – ....
6. miss ht williams – ....

4) Completing a form
Complete the form about you. Write about a sports centre or your own school.

- Surname: (1) ....
- First name: (2) ....
- Title: (3) .... Age: (4) ....
- Nationality: (5) ....
- Home town: (6) ....
- Occupation: (7) ....
- Interests: (8) ....
- Sports: (9) ....
- Class: (10) ....
- Time of classes: (11) ....
- Name of teacher: (12) ....

Playing sport 6

CHECK YOUR GRAMMAR AND VOCABULARY

1 can/can't
Complete the sentences with *can* or *can't*.
(1 mark each)

1 She's good at sports. She .... play tennis and basketball.
2 I'm good at basketball but I .... play tennis.
3 .... you ski? Yes, but not very well.
4 My brother is good at languages. He .... speak French, Italian and Spanish.
5 Are your friends good at sport? No, they .... swim, play tennis or basketball.
6 My parents .... speak English but not very well.

[6]

2 there is/there are, there isn't/there aren't
Complete the sentences with the correct form.
(0.5 marks each)

1 .... a sports centre in this town. It's very good.
2 The centre has got a big pool, but .... a children's pool.
3 .... swimming classes at this sports centre? Yes, ...
4 This sports centre is very good. .... classes every day.
5 The centre has got a gym, but .... aerobics classes.
6 .... a gym near here? Yes, ... It's in Green Street.

[4]

3 Circle the correct word. (0.5 marks each)

1 My favourite sport is *swim/swimming*.
2 I can *play/do* football very well.
3 Can you *do/jump* the long jump?
4 The basketball *pitch/court* is new.
5 My school hasn't got a football *court/pitch*.
6 I can *speak/talk* Spanish.

[3]

4 Adverbs
Circle the correct word in the second sentence.
(1 mark each)

1 I'm not very good at swimming.
   = I can swim but *very well/not very well*.
2 They're a fantastic football team.
   = They can play football *brilliantly/fast*.
3 I'm very good at English.
   = I can speak English *well/very well*.
4 He's a fast athlete.
   = He can run *fast/well*.

[4]

5 Times
Write the times. (0.5 marks each)

1 12:00 ....
2 7:45   ....
3 4:30   ....
4 9:20   ....
5 2:15   ....
6 8:55   ....

[3]

Check your progress

Choose the correct word. (1 mark each)

Todd: Welcome to the Play Well Sports Centre.
Sue: Thank you. (1) *This/These* centre is great! Is (2) *it/she* new?
Todd: Yes, and (3) *we/we've* got a fantastic swimming pool, twelve tennis courts and a big gym. What's (4) *you/your* favourite sport?
Sue: Tennis, but I (5) *can/can't* play very well. (6) *Are/Is* there tennis classes at (7) *a/the* sports centre?
Todd: Yes, there (8) *is/are*. They're (9) *at/in* 10.30 a.m. and 4.30 p.m.
Sue: And in the evening, too?
Todd: No, I'm sorry. There (10) *are/aren't* classes in the evening. Can you (11) *do/run* any other sports?
Sue: I can swim and dive.
Todd: There (12) *'s/are* a fantastic pool here. (13) *It's/Its* open from 10 a.m. to 9 p.m. every day.
Sue: (14) *What's/Where's* the time now?
Todd: It's 10.05.
Sue: Great! (15) *What's/Where's* the pool, please?

[15]

TOTAL: [35]

37

7 Every day

13 GRAMMAR

Present Simple + *I/you/we/they*

1 ★ **Affirmative**
Write the words in the correct order.

1 out/I/every/go/weekend.
   I go out every weekend.
2 friends./your/You/play/with/tennis
   ....
3 at/shopping/They/weekends./the/do
   ....
4 on/the/go/bus./centre/We/to/the/city
   ....
5 week./cinema/I/to/every/go/the
   ....

2 ★ **Affirmative**
Look at the pictures of the Davies family. Use them to complete sentences 1–6.

3 ★ **Negative**
Write the sentences in the negative.

1 We go to the cinema every week.
   We don't go to the cinema every week.
2 I have lunch at one o'clock.
   ....
3 You play basketball at weekends.
   ....
4 We read the newspaper every morning.
   ....
5 My parents do the shopping in the centre.
   ....
6 My brother and I do our homework every evening.
   ....

On Saturdays ...

1 My sister and I/at nine o'clock
   My sister and I get up at nine o'clock.
2 I/in the morning
   ....
3 My brothers/in the afternoon
   ....
4 We/at seven o'clock
   ....
5 We/in the evening
   ....
6 My parents/at eleven thirty
   ....

38

4 ★ Negative
Tick (✓) the correct sentence.

1. a) We not go out at weekends.
   b) We don't go out at weekends. ✓
2. a) I don't have lunch at school. ✓
   b) I'm not have lunch at school.
3. a) You no read the newspaper.
   b) You don't read the newspaper. ✓
4. a) They not go to the Internet café. ✓
   b) They don't go to the Internet café.

5 ★★ Affirmative and negative
Read about Gary's weekends. Complete the text with the correct form of the verbs in brackets.

My name's Gary. I (1) __live__ (live) in New York. My weekends are great! I (2) _____ (not go) to school and I (3) _____ (get up) late – at about ten o'clock. I (4) _____ (watch) TV with my sister in the morning. At two o'clock, we (5) _____ (have) lunch in a restaurant with my mum and dad. My parents (6) _____ (do) the shopping, but my sister and I (7) _____ (not go) with them. We (8) _____ (meet) our friends at an Internet café in the centre. What about you? Tell me about your weekend …

6 ★★ Affirmative and negative
Look at the pictures in Exercise 2. Write five true sentences about you in your notebook.

On Saturdays …
1. I _get up at ten o'clock._
2. I _____.
3. My friends and I _____.
4. My family and I _____.
5. My parents _____.

VOCABULARY

7 Days of the week
Find the days of the week. Look [→] and [↓].

T	H	U	R	S	D	M	O	N	D	A
H	R	S	A	T	M	O	B	W	Y	S
L	N	I	T	U	E	N	G	I	M	U
W	E	D	N	E	S	D	A	Y	S	N
E	S	W	Y	S	C	A	D	V	U	D
D	F	R	I	D	A	Y	I	R	D	A
L	N	F	S	A	T	U	R	D	A	Y
S	A	T	U	Y	G	J	O	L	Y	F
T	H	U	R	S	D	A	Y	G	P	R

8
Complete the sentences with the correct days.
1. Today is _____ .
2. _____ to _____ are schooldays.
3. _____ and _____ are the weekend.
4. We have English classes on _____ .
5. We have homework on _____ .

9 Prepositions
Write the words in the correct list in your notebook.

the evening, Fridays, my birthday, Saturdays, the afternoon, school days, the morning, Tuesday evenings, Monday afternoon, Wednesdays

in	on
the evening	Fridays

Now complete the rule with *in* or *on*.

We use __in__ with parts of days.
We use __on__ with days, or days + parts of days.

10 Routines
Circle the correct word.
1. I (go)/play swimming at weekends.
2. I go/get up at seven o'clock in the morning.
3. I do/make my homework every evening.
4. You don't watch/see TV in the mornings.
5. My parents make/do the shopping on Saturdays.
6. We have/take breakfast late at weekends.

7 Everyday

14 GRAMMAR
Present Simple + he/she/it

1 ★ **Affirmative**
Write the he/she/it form of the verbs.

1 clean *cleans*
2 play ....
3 teach ....
4 dance ....
5 watch ....
6 do ....
7 study ....
8 write ....

2 ★★ **Affirmative**
Read about John. Write the correct form of the verbs in brackets.

John (1) *gets up* (get up) at 7.30 a.m. He (2) .... (have) breakfast at 8.00 and then he (3) .... (go) to his office on the train. He (4) .... (read) the newspaper. He (5) .... (work) for a big company in London. In his job, he (6) .... (meet) people from other companies. He (7) .... (travel) to the USA on business every three weeks.

3 ★ **Negative**
Use the cues to write sentences.

1 my friend/not play tennis/at weekends
   My friend doesn't play tennis at weekends.
2 my sister/not study/English
   ....
3 Julia/not go to school/on Saturdays
   ....
4 my father/not work/at home
   ....
5 Martina/not go to bed/early
   ....
6 my mother/not make lunch/at weekends
   ....

4 ★ **Negative**
Tick (✓) the correct sentence.

1 a) Our cat doesn't sleep in the house. ✓
   b) Our cat not sleep in the house. ☐
2 a) The teacher doesn't lives near school. ☐
   b) The teacher doesn't live near school. ☐
3 a) Ana don't work in an office. ☐
   b) Ana doesn't work in an office. ☐
4 a) My sister doesn't study English. ☒
   b) My sister not study English. ☐

5 ★★ **Affirmative and negative**
Use the words to write sentences.

1 my father/not work in an office/ work in a clinic
   My father doesn't work in an office. He works in a clinic.
2 my mother/not translate texts/ write computer programs
   ....
3 she/not work in the morning/ work in the afternoon
   ....
4 my brother/not study/ work for a big company
   ....
5 my cat/not sleep on my bed/ sleep in the kitchen
   ....

6 ★★★ **Present Simple (all forms)**
Complete the text with the correct form of the verbs in brackets.

On school days, I (1) *get up* (get up) at 7.00 a.m. I (2) .... (have) breakfast with my mother and sister. We (3) .... (not see) my father in the morning – he (4) .... (go) to work very early. My sister and I (5) .... (go) to school on the bus. The school isn't near our house and we (6) .... (not go) home for lunch. In the evening, I (7) .... (watch) TV with my father, but my mother (8) .... (study).

At weekends, we (9) .... (have) more free time. My sister and I (10) .... (not go) to school. My father (11) .... (not work) and my mother (12) .... (not study). On Saturdays, we (13) .... (have) lunch in a nice restaurant. On Sundays, we (14) .... (visit) my grandparents. They (15) .... (live) in a beautiful house near the park.

Everyday 7

VOCABULARY

7 Routines
Write the correct verb under the pictures.

 Use the Mini-dictionary to help you.

1 ..*get up*.. 2 .... a shower

3 .... breakfast 4 .... your teeth

5 .... TV 6 .... to music

7 .... your homework 8 .... to bed

8
Where can you do the activities 2–7 in Exercise 7? Choose a room from the box and write true sentences in your notebook.

sitting room, bathroom, kitchen, bedroom

I do my homework in my bedroom.

9 Jobs
Complete the sentences with *a* or *an* and the words in the box.

nurse, secretary, student, musician, electrician, architect, waiter, fashion designer

1 ..*A nurse*.. looks after people in a hospital.
2 .... designs houses and offices.
3 .... brings food and drinks to people in a restaurant.
4 .... plays a musical instrument.
5 .... studies at university.
6 .... makes beautiful clothes.
7 .... repairs electrical machines.
8 .... types letters and answers the phone.

Check your answers in the Mini-dictionary.

Word Corner

Look at the underlined words. Are they nouns (N) or verbs (V)?

1 Do you <u>watch</u> TV at weekends? ☑ V
2 Have you got a <u>watch</u>? ☑ N
3 I don't <u>drink</u> coffee. ☐
4 Can I have a <u>drink</u>? ☐
5 <u>Call</u> us soon! ☐
6 Give me a <u>call</u>! ☐
7 There are two <u>phones</u> in my house. ☐
8 My friend <u>phones</u> every day. ☐
9 <u>Answer</u> all the questions. ☐
10 Write your <u>answer</u> here. ☐

Check your answers in the Mini-dictionary.

7 Everyday

Reading and Writing

1 Reading
Read the text. Are these sentences true (T) or false (F)?

1 Tony goes to school in Alice Springs.
2 Tony studies for six hours every school day.
3 Tony has lessons at the weekend.
4 Tony watches TV in the evening.

My name's Tony and I'm thirteen. I live in Australia. Our farm is very far from the town of Alice Springs. I get up at 7.00 a.m. I have breakfast with my mother. My father doesn't eat with us – he works on our farm.
 I don't go out to school. From mondays to fridays I study at home. Every week, I have three radio lessons from a school in Alice Springs. I don't have a teacher at home, but I study from 8 a.m. until 2 p.m. every school day. I use my computer and I ask my teacher questions in e-mails.
 I don't study in the afternoon, or on saturdays and sundays. After my lessons, I phone my friends. I play computer games. In the evening, we eat at 7 p.m. We watch TV for an hour. We go to bed at 9 p.m. – we get up early every day.

2 Punctuation: Capital letters
Look at these sentences from Tony's letter. Correct the mistakes with capital letters.

From mondays to fridays I study at home.
I don't study in the afternoon, or on saturdays and sundays.

3 Linking with *then*
Link these sentences with *then* in your notebook.

1 I get up at 7.00 a.m. I have breakfast with my mother.

I get up at 7.00 a.m. Then I have breakfast with my mother.

2 After my lessons, I phone my friends. I play computer games.
3 In the evening, we eat at 7 p.m. We watch TV for an hour.
4 I get up at half past eight. I have a shower.
5 We walk to school. We see our friends.
6 Helen goes home. She does her homework.
7 John has dinner at 8 p.m. He goes out.

4 Put these actions in the true order for you.
Write sentences with *then* in your notebook.

1 watch TV/do my homework
2 have a shower/have breakfast
3 see your friends/do your homework
4 read a book/go to bed

I do my homework. Then I watch TV.

5 Spelling
Correct these spelling mistakes.

1 busines *business*
2 Wensday
3 gitar
4 frend
5 swiming
6 intresting
7 brekfast
8 fayvourite

42

Check Your Grammar and Vocabulary

1 Present Simple
Circle the correct form. (0.5 marks each)

1. He *play/plays* sport every weekend.
2. She *goes/go* to school at 8 a.m.
3. We *don't/doesn't* meet friends every weekend.
4. They *don't work/not work* at weekends.
5. My father *don't/doesn't* have lunch at work.
6. I *doesn't/don't* drink tea.

[3]

2 Present Simple
Write the correct form of the verbs in brackets. (1 mark each)

1. I .... (clean) my bedroom every week.
2. My friend and I .... (not go) to school at weekends.
3. You .... (not get up) early at weekends.
4. They .... (do) the high jump.
5. Our cat .... (not sleep) in the house.
6. You .... (write) interesting letters.
7. I .... (not make) breakfast.

[7]

3 Routines and activities
Write the words in the box in the correct list. (0.5 marks each)

| tennis, out, the shopping, dinner, your homework, the guitar, swimming, a sandwich, a shower, to work, football, home |

play	go
....	....
....	....
....	....
	....

have	do
....	....
....	....
....	

[6]

4 Prepositions
Choose the correct word. (0.5 marks each)

1. I go to the Internet café *on/in* Saturdays.
2. He reads the newspaper *on/in* the morning.
3. Fiona works *on/in* the evening.
4. I get up early *on/in* schooldays.

[2]

5 Days of the week
Write the letters in the correct order. Add capital letters where necessary. (0.5 marks each)

1. asutedy ....
2. sednweday ....
3. ydhrtusa ....
4. adaustry ....

[2]

Check your progress

Choose the correct word. (1 mark each)

I (1) *am/is* a student. I (2) *study/studies* medicine at the university in my town. I (3) *live/lives* with my parents in (4) *a/the* house near the city centre. I (5) *have/has* got a sister, but she (6) *doesn't/don't* live in (7) *a/the* house. She's (8) *a/an* architect and she (9) *work/works* in London. (10) *His/Her* job is very interesting. My parents (11) *is/are* teachers in the same school. My mum (12) *teach/teaches* French. My dad is (13) *a/an* art teacher and he (14) *paints/paint* in (15) *his/her* free time.

[15]

TOTAL: [35]

8 Free time

15 GRAMMAR
Present Simple questions

1 ★ *Yes/No questions*
Complete the questions with *do* or *does*.

1 *Do* I speak English well?
2 .... you collect things?
3 .... she surf the Internet?
4 .... your parents go dancing?
5 .... Ana do her homework every evening?
6 .... we buy clothes every week?
7 .... Andy listen to soul?
8 .... they go out every evening?

2 ★★ *Yes/No questions and short answers*
Look at the table. Write questions and short answers.

	📷	🎹	💻	🖂
Jane	✓	✗	✓	✗
Nick	✗	✓	✓	✗
Rachel	✓	✓	✓	✓
Paul	✗	✗	✓	✗

1 Jane/take photos?
   Does Jane take photos? Yes, she does.
2 Jane and Paul/play the piano?
   Do Jane and Paul play the piano?
   No, they don't.
3 Paul/use a computer?
   .... ? ....
4 Jane/collect stamps?
   .... ? ....
5 Nick and Paul/take photos?
   .... ? ....
6 Rachel/collect stamps?
   .... ? ....
7 Nick and Rachel/play the piano?
   .... ? ....
8 Jane, Nick, Rachel and Paul/use a computer?
   .... ? ....

3 ★ *Wh- questions*
Complete the questions with the question words.

What, How often, Where, When

1 *What* films do you watch?
   Action films.
2 .... does he play the guitar?
   In his bedroom.
3 .... sports do you play?
   Basketball and tennis.
4 .... do they go swimming?
   Once a week.
5 .... does Emma go dancing?
   On Friday evenings.

4 ★★ *Present Simple + Wh- questions*
Write questions for these answers.

1 *How often do you go fishing?*
   I go fishing twice a month.
2 ....
   They play football at school.
3 ....
   I go to bed at 10.30.
4 ....
   We listen to heavy metal and soul.
5 ....
   They eat sandwiches for lunch.
6 ....
   She does her homework in the sitting room.
7 ....
   He watches TV every day.
8 ....
   She gets up at 7.30.

Free time 8

5 ★★★ *Yes/No* and *Wh-* questions
Write questions for the survey.

FREE TIME SURVEY

1 you/go shopping?
   Do you go shopping?
2 Where/you/go shopping?
   ....
3 What/you/buy?
   ....
4 your friend/play sport?
   ....
5 What/he,she/play?
   ....
6 your parents/use a computer?
   ....
7 they/surf the Internet?
   ....
8 How often/you and your family/go out?
   ....
9 Where/you/go?
   ....

6 ★★★ Answer the survey questions in your notebook.

VOCABULARY

7 Free time
Write the names of the activities under the pictures.

go dancing, draw pictures, listen to music,
surf the Internet, read books, go fishing,
play computer games, watch videos

1 *go dancing*

2 ....

3 ....

4 ....

5 ....

6 ....

7 ....   8 ....

Check your answers in the Mini-dictionary.

8 What are your five favourite activities in Exercise 7? Number them. (1 = your favourite).

9 Frequency
Look at the table and complete the sentences about Anita.

activity	day	week	month	year
1 read the newspaper	1			
2 go to the cinema		1		
3 play tennis			2	
4 go swimming		2		
5 go to a museum				3

1 Anita *reads the newspaper once a day*.
2 She ....
3 She ....
4 She ....
5 She ....

10 Write these things in your notebook:
• five things you do every day
• three things you do every week
• two things you do every month

1 *I watch TV every day.*

8 Free time

16 GRAMMAR
like/don't like

1 ★ like/likes + noun
Write sentences.

1 I/ ⚽
   I like football.

2 You/ 🎾
   ....

3 My friend/ 🏫
   ....

4 She/ 🥛
   ....

5 My brother and I/ 🥪
   ....

6 My parents/ 🎵
   ....

2 ★ don't/doesn't like + noun
Complete the sentences.

1 I *don't like* dogs.
2 My sister .... science fiction films.
3 My friends and I .... history lessons.
4 You .... coffee.
5 They .... soul music.
6 He .... American films.

3 ★ Yes/No and Wh- questions
Write questions.

1 you/school?
   Do you like school?
2 What/lessons/you?
   What lessons do you like?
3 your friend/sport?
   ....
4 your parents/the cinema?
   ....
5 What films/you?
   ....
6 your friends/computer games?
   ....

4 ★★ All forms
Complete the text with the correct form of *like* or short answers.

Adam: (1) Do you *like* music?
Bella: Oh, yes, I (2) ....
Adam: What music (3) .... you .... ?
Bella: Well, I listen to Latin music and I also (4) .... soul.
Adam: And heavy metal?
Bella: Oh, no! I (5) .... heavy metal. It's terrible! But my brother (6) .... it. He listens to heavy metal every day.
Adam: (7) .... your parents .... heavy metal?
Bella: No, they (8) .... They (9) .... classical music.

5 ★ -ing
Write the *-ing* forms. Then match them with the correct rule.

1 go   *going*
2 dance *dancing*
3 run   *running*
4 play   *playing*
5 write ....
6 collect ....
7 make   ....
8 get   ....
9 read   ....
10 swim ....
11 take ....
12 draw ....

Rules

1 Most verbs, verbs ending in -y/w: + -ing
   going   *playing*   ....

2 Verbs ending in one -e: ~~e~~ + -ing
   dancing   ....

3 One syllable verbs with one vowel + one consonant: **consonant x 2 + -ing**
   running   ....

6 ★ like + -ing
Complete the sentences with the correct form of *like* and the *-ing* form of the verbs in the box.

play, have, write, collect, watch, dance

1 I *like playing* sport.
2 My friends and I .... at the disco.
3 He .... letters to his penfriend.
4 My brother .... stamps.
5 My parents .... lunch in a restaurant at weekends.
6 You .... action films.

Free time 8

7 ★★ like/don't like + -ing
Write sentences.

1 I/like/swim (✓) /I/like/play tennis (✗)
   I like swimming but I don't like playing tennis.
2 We/like/listen to music (✓) /we/like/watch TV (✗)
   ....
3 He/like/use his computer (✓) /he/like/surf the Internet (✗)
   ....
4 They/like/watch videos (✓) /they/like/go to the cinema (✗)
   ....
5 My sister/like/swim (✓) /she/like/dive (✗)
   ....
6 You/like/draw (✓) /you/like/paint (✗)
   ....

8 ★★ Questions and answers
Write questions and true short answers.

1 you/like/study?
   Do you like studying?
   Yes, I do. / No, I don't.
2 your friend/like/go to museums
   ....? ....
3 your parents/like/watch videos
   ....? ....
4 you/like/buy clothes
   ....? ....
5 you and your friends/like/do athletics
   ....? ....
6 you/like/draw
   ....? ....

VOCABULARY

9 Prepositions
Complete the sentences with *to*, *to the* or no preposition.

1 I want to go *to the* museum.
2 We don't go .... bed early.
3 My dad goes .... fishing every week.
4 I go .... swimming once a week.
5 My friends go .... city centre on Saturdays.
6 We go .... school at 8.30 a.m.

10 like, love, don't like, hate
Write sentences with the correct form of the verbs.

✓ = like   ✓✓ = love
✗ = don't like   ✗✗ = hate

1 I/ ✓✓
   I love swimming.
2 We/ ✗✗
   ....
3 Steve/ ✓
   ....
4 They/ ✗
   ....
5 You/ ✗✗
   ....
6 Sue/ ✓✓
   ....

11 Prices
Circle the correct form.

1 (twenty-five pence)/
   twenty-five pounds   **25p**

2 one pound fifty pence/
   one pound fifty   **£1.50**

3 seventeen pounds thirty-five/
   seventy pounds thirty-five   **£17.35**

4 forty-eight pounds fifteen/
   forty-eight pounds fifty   **£48.50**

5 ninety-nine pounds/
   ninety-nine pounds ninety-nine   **£99.99**

Word Corner

Underline the adjectives in these sentences.

1 I like <u>historic</u> cities and <u>interesting</u> museums.
2 There is a new cinema and a fantastic sports centre.
3 Do you like English or American music?
4 Have you got any T-shirts? Small or large?
5 I think salsa music is horrible and soul is great.

Check your answers in the Mini-dictionary.

8 Free time

Reading and Writing

1 Letter layout
Write the numbers on the correct part of the letter.

1. Write soon!
2. 12/05/02
3. Please write to me and tell me about the things you like.
4. My name is Mark. I'm from Birmingham — a city in the centre of England. I'm sixteen years old. My mother is a computer programmer and my father is an electrician. I've got a brother called Andy and a sister called Diane.
5. Mark
6. Dear Antonio,
7. 42 Victoria Road
   Birmingham
   UK
8. I love football. My favourite team is Aston Villa. I go to football matches every weekend with my friends and I like playing football at school. I also like going to the cinema. I love action films and my favourite actor is Bruce Willis. I hate westerns! Do you like westerns?

2 Read the letter in the correct order and answer these questions in your notebook.

1. Where is Mark from?
2. How old is he?
3. How many children are there in his family?
4. What does Mark like doing?
5. What does he hate?
6. Do you like the same things as Mark?

3 Punctuation: Addresses
Add punctuation to the address in Mark's letter.

42, Victoria Road,

4 Put the correct punctuation in these addresses.

1. 21 Church Street
   Manchester
   England

2. 15 Green Road
   Cambridge
   UK

5 Spelling
Correct the spelling mistakes.

1. foto
2. sandwitch
3. arcitect
4. chower
5. graf
6. kithen
7. booksop
8. lunsh
9. alfabet
10. T-chirt

6 Write the words from Exercise 5 in the correct list.

ph	sh	ch
photo		

Free time 8

CHECK YOUR GRAMMAR AND VOCABULARY

1 Present Simple questions
Complete the questions. (1 mark each)

1 How often .... (you/go) to the cinema?
2 .... (they/get up) early at weekends?
3 What .... (Simon/study) at university?
4 When .... (we/have) lunch?
5 .... (she/use) a computer at school?

[5]

2 like/don't like + -ing
Complete the sentences with the correct form of the verbs in brackets. (1 mark each)

1 .... she .... classical music? (like)
2 I .... basketball. (not like)
3 We love .... (dance)
4 Do you like .... to the theatre? (go)
5 The children hate .... early. (get up)

[5]

3 Frequency
Rewrite the expressions. (0.5 marks each)

1 one day in a week = ...
2 two times in a month = ...
3 all the days in a week = ...
4 all the months in a year = ...

[2]

4 Free time
Match the verbs and the nouns in the box. Some verbs have more than one noun. (0.5 marks each)

stamps, dancing, computer games, fishing, photos, football, music, videos

1 go ....
2 take ....
3 watch ....
4 play ....
5 collect ....
6 listen to ....

[4]

5 Prices
Write these prices in words. (0.5 marks each)

1 £1.75 ....
2 £15.99 ....
3 £34.68 ....
4 £50.27 ....

[2]

6 Prepositions
Complete the sentences with *to*, *to the* or no preposition. (0.5 marks)

1 I go .... home at 4.30.
2 They go .... cinema every week.
3 What time do you go .... school?
4 She goes .... dancing after school.

[2]

Check your progress

Circle the correct word in Dialogues 1 and 2. (1 mark each)

Dialogue 1
Paula: Hi! My name's Paula. I'm (1) *a/the* student at the university.
John: Oh, I (2) *goes/go* to the university, too. My name's John.
Paula: (3) *What/Where* do you study?
John: Maths. And you?
Paula: English literature. My brother (4) *study/studies* maths.
John: Oh, what's (5) *her/his* name?
Paula: Richard Evans.

Dialogue 2
John: I want to buy (6) *any/some* books.
(7) *Are/Is* there any good bookshops
(8) *near/to* the university?
Paula: Yes. Simpsons Bookshop is very good. It (9) *has/have* got hundreds of new books and (10) *their/they're* all cheap.
John: Great! Is (11) *it/she* open now?
Paula: Yes. It's open (12) *once/every* day from 9.00 to 6.00. What books do you want to buy?
John: Books about the cinema. I love (13) *watch/watching* films. Do you (14) *like/liking* the cinema?
Paula: Oh, yes. (15) *It's/Its* great!

[15]

TOTAL: [35]

9 Excursions

17 GRAMMAR
Present Continuous

1 ★ **Affirmative**
Write the verbs. Use full forms.

1 I *am watching* (watch) a video.
2 You .... (study).
3 They .... (swim) in the pool.
4 My sister .... (write) to her penfriend.
5 My friends and I .... (do) our homework.
6 The children .... (dance) to the music.
7 James .... (listen to) a CD.
8 The dog .... (eat) in the kitchen.

2 ★ **Affirmative**
Write the sentences in Exercise 1 with short forms where possible, in your notebook.

> 1 I'm watching a video.

3 ★ **Negative**
Write the sentences in the negative. Use short forms.

1 He is eating a sandwich.
   He isn't eating a sandwich.
2 I am doing my homework.
   ....
3 You are running fast.
   ....
4 We are playing basketball.
   ....
5 Helen is having a shower.
   ....
6 My mother is using the computer.
   ....
7 My parents are making lunch.
   ....
8 The cat is sleeping.
   ....

4 ★★ **Affirmative and negative**
Look at the picture. Correct the information in the sentences (1–7) and write them in your notebook.

1 Sue and Dan are watching TV.
   Sue and Dan aren't watching TV.
   They are listening to music.
2 Tom is eating.
3 Lynn is watching TV.
4 John and Andy are talking to friends.
5 Jane is listening to music.
6 Pete is watching a video.
7 The cats are eating.

Excursions 9

5 ★★ Affirmative and negative
Put the verbs in the Present Continuous.
Use short forms.

Julia: Hello?
Tim: Hi, Julia! It's Tim here. Where are you?
Julia: I'm at my grandmother's house.
(1) I *'m doing* (do) my homework. My parents aren't at home. (2) They .... (do) the shopping. Where are you?
Tim: I'm at the Internet café with Simon.
(3) We .... (surf) the Internet.
Julia: Lucky you! Is Helen with you?
Tim: No, (4) she .... (play) tennis.
Julia: Is she with Diana?
Tim: No, (5) Diana .... (not play) tennis today. (6) She .... (visit) her family.
Julia: All my friends (7) .... (relax) today and (8) I .... (study)!
Tim: Well, we (9) .... (not do) much, but come to the Internet café.
Julia: OK. See you in fifteen minutes.

VOCABULARY

6 Places
Complete the sentences with the words in the box.

castle, beach, market, museum, nature reserve, palace, art gallery

1 A *castle* is a very big, strong building.
2 There are paintings in an ....
3 People relax on the ....
4 A king or queen lives in a ....
5 People go shopping at a ....
6 There are statues and interesting objects in a ....
7 Animals live in a ....

7 Transport
Match the words (1–6) with the pictures (a–f).

1 plane   a)
2 bus   b)
3 taxi   c)
4 train   d)
5 coach   e)
6 car   f)

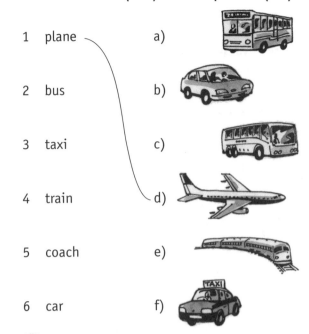

8 Prepositions
Circle the correct word.

1 We're sitting (in)/at/on a taxi (in)/on/at Manchester.
2 They are in/at/on home in/at/on their bedroom.
3 She isn't in/at/on the bus. She's in/at/on the train.
4 My sister is in/at/on school in/at/on her classroom.
5 He isn't in/at/on bed. He's watching TV.

9 Activities
In your notebook, write eight sentences about the people in the picture. Use the words in the box.

sitting in a taxi, eating a banana, looking at a map, taking photos, walking, talking on the phone, sightseeing, reading a guidebook

9 Excursions

18 GRAMMAR
Present Continuous questions

1 ★ *Yes/No questions*
Write questions.

1 you/clean/your room?
   Are you cleaning your room?
2 your brother/use/his computer?
   ....
3 she/wear/jeans and a T-shirt?
   ....
4 they/sightsee in the city?
   ....
5 it/rain?
   ....
6 we/go home/now?
   ....

2 ★★ *Yes/No questions and answers*
Complete the questions and write true short answers.

1 *Are* you *sitting* in your bedroom? (sit)
   Yes, I am./No, I'm not.
2 .... your teacher .... ? (talk)
   ....
3 .... you .... jeans? (wear)
   ....
4 .... your friends .... basketball? (play)
   ....
5 .... you .... a pen? (use)
   ....
6 .... your friend .... with you? (study)
   ....

3 ★ *Wh- questions*
Write questions for the answers.

1 Q: *What are you studying?*
   A: We're studying science.
2 Q: .... ?
   A: I'm wearing jeans and a T-shirt.
3 Q: .... ?
   A: My sister is talking to her friend.
4 Q: .... ?
   A: My friend is reading a magazine.
5 Q: .... ?
   A: My parents are eating sandwiches.
6 Q: .... ?
   A: I'm sitting on the bed in my bedroom.

4 ★★ *Yes/No and Wh- questions*
Write questions. Then match the answers (a–f).

Questions
1 What/he/do
  What is he doing? ☐ *a*
2 How/she/travel
  .... ☐
3 they/sightsee/in the city
  .... ☐
4 What/the dog/do
  .... ☐
5 your sister/wear/new clothes
  .... ☐
6 Who/you/write to
  .... ☐

Answers
a) He's watching a video.
b) No, she isn't.
c) My penfriend in Canada.
d) Yes, they are.
e) It's sleeping in the garden.
f) By train.

5 ★★ *All forms*
Complete the dialogue with the verbs in the box.

look at, take, ski, listen to, sit, wear, read, do, make, snow

Ann: I've got some new photos here.
Ben: Great!
Ann: This is our school excursion to the museum. (1) I *'m looking at* some ancient objects. And this is our teacher. (2) She .... a guidebook about the museum.
Ben: Who are the people near your teacher?
Ann: I don't know. I think they're tourists – (3) they .... photos. And this is my party.
Ben: What (4) .... Karen .... in this photo?
Ann: She's dancing to heavy metal music!
Ben: She's crazy! And (5) .... you .... a hat in this photo?
Ann: Yes, I am! I like my hat!
Ben: Where (6) .... you .... in this photo?
Ann: In my garden. (7) We .... music. Look at my mum here. (8) She .... lunch.
Ben: And who's this? I can't see very well. (9) It .... and very cold.
Ann: That's you! (10) You .... in the mountains!

Excursions 9

VOCABULARY

6 Clothes
Write the names of the clothes.

Use your Mini-dictionary.

Emma

1 ....
2 ....
3 ....

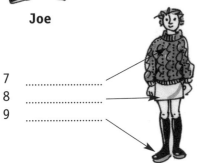
Joe

4 ....
5 ....
6 ....

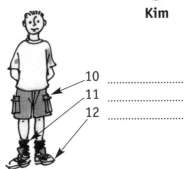
Kim

7 ....
8 ....
9 ....

Matt

10 ....
11 ....
12 ....

Sue

13 ....
14 ....
15 ....

7 Put the words in the correct list.
T-shirt, jeans, trainers, dress, trousers, socks, shirt, sandals, jacket, hat

a + noun	noun
a T-shirt	jeans
....	....
....	....
....	....
....	....

8 Correct the descriptions of Emma, Joe and Kim below and write a description of Matt and Sue.

1 Emma is wearing jeans, a shirt, shoes and a hat.
   Emma is wearing jeans, a T-shirt, trainers and a hat.
2 Joe is wearing jeans, a shirt and boots.
   ....
3 Kim is wearing a shirt, a jumper and shoes.
   ....
4 Matt ....
5 Sue ....

9 What clothes do you like?
Write sentences with *like*, *don't like*, *love* and *hate* in your notebook.

I like jeans and T-shirts.

Word Corner

Use your Mini-dictionary to help you.

1 Match the underlined words (1–6) to the types of word (a–f).

1 We <u>are sitting</u> in the garden.   a) noun
2 I love my <u>black</u> jeans.   b) adjective
3 Do you like <u>museums</u>?   c) verb
4 I can run <u>fast</u>.   d) linking word
5 Go to the market <u>but</u> don't go to the shops. e) preposition
6 Is there a bank <u>near</u> here?   f) adverb

2 Find these words in the Mini-dictionary. What type of word can they be?

1 phone *noun, verb*   4 love ....
2 hard   .... 5 orange ....
3 call   ....

53

9 Excursions

Reading and Writing

1) Reading
What do you know about Edinburgh? Answer these questions before you read the text. Write T (true) or F (false).

1. Edinburgh is the capital of Wales. ☐
2. Edinburgh hasn't got a castle. ☐
3. There is a festival in Edinburgh. ☐

2) Read *In the city* and check your answers.

> **Edinburgh**
>
> **In the city**
> Edinburgh, capital city of Scotland, is fantastic for sightseeing.
> - Walk around the streets and see the different styles of architecture. Don't miss the historic Old Town with its castle museums cathedral and arts centre.
> - The New Town is the place for shopping. Buy clothes food presents and souvenirs in the modern shops.
> - Edinburgh is famous for its festival. Every year people see shows plays and films and listen to different types of music – pop folk jazz and rock.
>
> **Excursions**
> - Visit the small town of North Berwick near Edinburgh. It's on the coast and it's got fantastic beaches with plants birds and animals. Don't miss the ancient ruins of Tantallon Castle.
> - Relax in the quiet villages along the coast (e.g. Dirleton and Gullane). Go walking sightseeing play golf or visit the gardens.

3) Read the rest of the text and choose the best picture a, b, c or d for *In the city*: Picture ☐ *Excursions*: Picture ☐

4) Read the text again and answer the questions.
1. Where is the castle in Edinburgh?
2. Are there shops in the Old Town?
3. How often is the Edinburgh Festival?
4. Where is North Berwick?
5. Is Tantallon Castle very old?
6. Are Dirleton and Gullane towns?

5) Punctuation: Commas
Correct the text. Put commas where necessary.

> Don't miss the historic Old Town with its castle, museums, cathedral and arts centre.

6) Write sentences in your notebook about the places to see in your town/city. Put commas where necessary.

> My city has got a nature reserve, an ancient cathedral and a castle.

7) Spelling
Write vowels (a, e, i, o, u) to complete the names of the cities.

1. Pr _a_ g _u_ _e_
2. W _ rs _ w
3. V _ _ nn _
4. M _ sc _ w
5. _ th _ ns
6. B _ rc _ l _ n _
7. B _ _ n _ s _ _ r _ s
8. M _ l _ n

Check Your Grammar and Vocabulary

1 Present Continuous
Write the verbs with short forms. (1 mark each)

1 It .... (not rain) now.
2 I .... (phone) my parents.
3 We .... (not go) to bed now.
4 He .... (run) along the road.
5 You .... (not eat) very much.

☐ 5

2 Present Continuous questions
Write questions. (1 mark each)

1 you/study?
....
2 Where/she/travel?
....
3 your parents/work/today?
....
4 Who/you/write to?
....
5 he/take/a shower?
....

☐ 5

3 Clothes, places and transport
Write the words in the correct list.
(0.5 marks each)

art gallery, train, skirt, beach, T-shirt, shoes, palace, shorts, coach, jumper

Clothes	Places
....	....
....	....
....	....
....	

Transport
....
....

☐ 5

4 Activities
Choose the correct word. (0.5 marks each)

1 Do you like *taking/making* photos?
2 They're *saying/talking* on the phone.
3 I'm *looking/seeing* at a map.
4 She's *drinking/eating* a sandwich.

☐ 2

5 Prepositions
Complete the sentences with *by*, *on*, *at* or *in*.
(0.5 marks each)

1 My mum goes to work .... foot.
2 Is your brother .... home?
3 We're sitting .... a coach.
4 Do you go to school .... bus?
5 The family is .... the garden.
6 I don't like going .... train.

☐ 3

Check your progress

Circle the correct word. (1 mark each)

Dear Hannah,

Mum and I (1) **is/are** in New York! We (2) **is/are** sitting near the swimming pool (3) **in/on** the hotel. She (4) **are/is** listening to music and we are both (5) **relax/relaxing**.

New York is fantastic! It (6) **have/has** got (7) **some/any** interesting places and (8) **a/the** big park. We (9) **go/going** to the centre every day (10) **in/by** taxi. Mum loves (11) **look/looking** at the paintings in the museums and galleries.

There (12) **is/are** also some fantastic shops in the city. (13) **It's/Its** clothes shops have got nice jeans and T-shirts. (14) **Are/Do** you like clothes from the USA? I think (15) **they're/their** great.

See you soon!

Andrea

☐ 15

TOTAL: ☐ 35

10 Wildlife

19 GRAMMAR

must/mustn't

1 ★ **must**

What are the people saying? Match the sentences with the pictures.

1 You must buy some new clothes. `b`
2 You must do your homework.
3 You must eat your dinner.
4 You must clean the kitchen.
5 You must go to bed.

2 ★★ **must**

Write instructions with *must* about an animal project. Then put the sentences in the correct order (1–4).

Then you/write notes/about the animal
☐ *Then you must write notes about the animal.*

Finally, you/check/your spelling and punctuation.
☐ ....
....

Then you/write/your description.
☐ ....

First, you/choose/an animal
☐ ....

3 ★ **mustn't**

Look at the signs. Write sentences with *mustn't* and the verbs in the box.

drop litter, go near the dog, take photos, smoke, swim

1 *You mustn't drop litter.*

2 ....

3 ....

4 ....

5 ....

Wildlife 10

4 ★★ must/mustn't
Write sentences about the rules for an English exam in your notebook.

1 Write your name on the paper. ✓
2 Copy from other students. ✗
3 Write in pen. ✓
4 Use a dictionary. ✗
5 Talk in the exam room. ✗
6 Answer all the questions. ✓
7 Give your paper to the teacher. ✓

1 You must write your name on the paper.
2 You mustn't copy from other students.

5 ★★★ must/mustn't
Write four rules for your class in your notebook.

You must listen to the teacher.
You mustn't eat in the classroom.

VOCABULARY

6 Animals
Find eleven animals in the box.

Y	W	U	W	O	L	F	L	I	O	A
H	I	P	P	O	K	O	A	I	S	D
G	B	Y	E	B	R	L	L	A	M	A
E	R	A	N	S	H	H	I	K	M	Z
K	A	N	G	A	R	O	O	Y	X	E
O	E	D	U	F	V	I	N	E	L	B
A	X	T	I	G	E	R	K	M	O	R
L	G	I	N	M	O	P	A	N	D	A
A	G	V	E	L	E	P	H	A	N	T

7 Write the animals in the plural in your notebook.
Which word is irregular? ....

8 Adjectives
Match the adjectives (1–5) with the definitions (a–e).

1 friendly — e
2 huge
3 interesting
4 lovely
5 rare

a describes animals that are very difficult to see or hear
b describes something that makes you want to listen or watch
c describes something very big
d describes something very pleasant or enjoyable
e describes someone who is kind and pleasant

9 Complete the sentences with the adjectives from Exercise 8.

1 Animals aren't boring. I think they are very <u>interesting</u>.
2 Elephants aren't big – they are ....
3 Are tigers ....? Yes, there aren't many tigers in the world now.
4 Golden eagles aren't horrible. I think they're ....
5 Chimps live in families and they are very ....

10 Prepositions
Write three sentences about the animals in your notebook. Use *next to* or *near*.

The camel is next to the elephant.

11 Circle the correct word.
1 We go *to*/*at* the wildlife park every year.
2 We're going to the zoo *in*/*by* coach.
3 Look at the hippo. It's *in*/*on* the water.
4 Koalas live *in*/*to* Australia.
5 The wildlife park has got animals *at*/*from* different countries.
6 You must go to the forest *on*/*by* foot.

10 Wildlife

20 GRAMMAR
Subject and object pronouns, possessive adjectives

1 ★ **Subject and object pronouns**
Complete the table.

Subject pronouns	Object pronouns
I	me
....	you
he	....
....	her
it	....
we	....
....	them

2 ★ **Object pronouns**
Complete the sentences.

1 My brother is doing his homework. I'm helping *him* .
2 Dogs are horrible. I don't like ....
3 I want to call my friend. Pass .... the phone, please.
4 Mum is making lunch. You must help ....
5 My grandfather knows about other countries. Ask .... about Australia.
6 You are very nice. I like ....
7 Our teacher gives .... homework every day.
8 The cat is hungry. You must feed ....

3 ★ **Subject and object pronouns**
Circle the correct word.

1 Give *I/(me)* your phone number.
2 That house is fantastic. Look at *it/him*!
3 I've got two cats. *They/Them* are lovely.
4 Tell *we/us* about those animals.
5 My sister is twelve. *Her/She* likes animals.
6 Pass *he/him* the guidebook, please.
7 *We/Us* want to go to the wildlife park.
8 These books are new. Put *they/them* on the shelf.

4 ★★ **Object pronouns**
Write sentences in your notebook. Add the correct object pronoun.

1 history – interesting. I/like
2 computers – great. I/love
3 football – boring. I/hate
4 exams – terrible. I/hate
5 swimming – fantastic. I/love
6 zoos – boring. I/not like

> 1 *History is interesting. I like it.*

5 ★★ **Object pronouns**
Write your opinion about the things using the adjectives in the box. Write another sentence with *like/don't like* and an object pronoun.

> great, interesting, boring, horrible

1 geography
   Geography is interesting. I like it.
2 dogs
   Dogs are horrible. I don't like them.
3 jeans
   ....
4 art
   ....
5 action movies
   ....
6 literature
   ....
7 museums
   ....

6 ★★ **Subject/object pronoun or possessive adjective?**
Circle the correct word.

(1) *I/(My)/Me* name's Leo and I love animals. I think (2) *them/they/their* are very interesting. My favourite animals are tigers. I love (3) *them/they/their* colours. (4) *They/Them/Their* are very rare now but there are some tigers in the wildlife park near my town. I like visiting (5) *them/they/their* every week. My favourite is the baby. (6) *It/Its/It's* is about two years old and (7) *its/it's/it* eyes are lovely. My girlfriend likes animals, too. (8) *Her/She/His* favourite animals are dolphins. She loves (9) *their/them/they* – and she loves (10) *me/I/my* , too!

58

Wildlife 10

7 ★★ Write the description again with pronouns and possessive adjectives instead of the underlined words.

My brother, Tom, and I are doing a project. Our dad is helping us.

My brother Tom and I are doing a project. Tom's and my dad is helping Tom and me. The project is about animals and the project is very interesting. Tom and I like animals but Tom and I don't know very much about animals. Dad is a teacher and Dad knows about rare animals. Tom and I ask Dad questions and Dad gives Tom and me information. Dad, Tom and I make notes and then write descriptions of the animals. Jenny, Tom's and my sister, likes art and we put Jenny's drawings with Tom's and my descriptions.

VOCABULARY

8 Parts of an animal
Label the animals. Use the words in the box.

body (x2), head, ear, eye, leg, wing, neck, tail, foot

9 Match the descriptions and the pictures. Then write the names of the animals.

a) It's grey. It lives in Africa. It can swim. It's got a huge body. It's got small eyes and ears.
b) It's got a long body and a small head. It hasn't got legs. It is very intelligent and friendly. It can swim brilliantly.
c) It's black and white. It lives in Africa. It's got a tail. It can run fast.
d) It eats leaves. It has got a very long neck and four long legs. It can run fast.

1 c .... 2 ☐ ....

3 ☐ .... 4 ☐ ....

10 Write a description of your favourite animal in your notebook.

Word Corner

Use your Mini-dictionary to help you.

1 Underline the pronouns.

1 <u>I</u> like studying animals. <u>They</u> are interesting.
2 The teacher is talking. Listen to <u>her</u>.
3 Look at the animals but don't feed them.
4 That's a male. He's very big. Don't touch him.
5 We don't know the answer. Please tell us.
6 This is a koala. It's from Australia. Take a photo of it.

2 Write the nouns in brackets in the plural.

1 They are *businessmen* (businessman)
2 The .... like the zoo. (child)
3 Look at those .... (wolf)
4 That rabbit has got big .... (foot)
5 I like interesting .... (person)
6 Clean your .... now. (tooth)
7 They are their .... (wife)
8 Koalas eat .... (leaf)

10 Wildlife

Reading and Writing

1 Reading
Read the text. Are these sentences true (T) or false (F)?

1 European bison live in all parts of Europe. ☐
2 Baby bison live with the females. ☐
3 Males and females live in the same group. ☐
4 Wolves eat bison. ☐

European Bison (bison bonasus)

european bison are rare now. Where do (1) <u>they</u> live. What colour are they. What do they eat.

European bison live in forests in poland. (2) <u>They</u> are brown they are big animals (2.9 m long and 800–1000 kg) they have got big bodies short necks and long tails. They havent got very long legs. European bison cant run fast. They can jump.

European bison in the wild live to about 27 years old. (3) <u>They</u> eat grass and leaves. They feed about five times a day. They sleep or play. The females live in groups of about 20. The babies live with (4) <u>them</u>. The males live alone or in small groups. wolves live near the bison and sometimes hunt (5) <u>them</u>.

2 Look at the underlined words. What nouns do they refer to?

1 _European bison_
2 ....
3 ....
4 ....
5 ....

3 Punctuation: Question marks
Correct the text. Add question marks (?) where necessary.

> Where do they live?

4 Write the words in the correct order to make questions. Add capital letters and question marks (?).

1 pumas/do/what/eat
   What do pumas eat?
2 Africa/tigers/live/in/do
   ....
3 do/where/from/come/eagles
   ....
4 park/the/you/are/to/going/wildlife
   ....
5 go/often/how/you/zoo/do/the/to
   ....
6 animal/are/what/you/at/looking
   ....

5 Punctuation: Review
Correct the text. Add capital letters, apostrophes (') commas (,) and full stops (.) where necessary.

6 Linking with *but* and *then*
Link these sentences with *but* or *then*.

1 European bison can't run fast. They can jump.
   European bison can't run fast but they can jump.
2 They feed every day. They sleep or play.
   Thye feed every day. Then they sleep or play.
3 Finish your description. Check it.
   ....
4 It's a small animal. It's very strong.
   ....
5 Look at the birds. Don't touch them.
   ....
6 You must finish the test. Give it to your teacher.
   ....

Wildlife 10

CHECK YOUR GRAMMAR AND VOCABULARY

1) must/mustn't
Complete the sentences with *must* or *mustn't*.
(0.5 marks each)

1 I'm studying. You .... play music.
2 It's very late. You .... go to bed.
3 People are watching a film. You .... use your mobile phone.
4 The baby is sleeping. You .... touch her.
5 Today is a schoolday. You .... get up early.
6 This is a test. You .... copy.
7 It's very cold. You .... wear a jumper.
8 The dog is hungry. You .... feed it.

☐ 4

2) Object pronouns
Complete the sentences with an object pronoun.
(1 mark each)

1 You are a very interesting person. We like ....
2 My brother is an actor. Do you know .... ?
3 We don't understand. Please help ....
4 I've got a guitar but I can't play .... very well.
5 She loves her grandparents. She visits .... every week.
6 That panda is a female. Look at ....
7 I love your letters. Please write to .... soon.

☐ 7

3) Write the words in the correct list.
(0.5 marks each)

wolf, rare, tiger, ear, llama, wing, eye, huge, friendly, lion, head, eagle, koala, interesting, tail, lovely, foot, panda

Animals	Parts of animals
....	....
....	....
....	....
....	....
....	....
....	....

Adjectives
....
....
....
....
....

☐ 9

Check your progress

Circle the correct word. (1 mark each)

Ella: What are you (1) *do/doing*?
Pete: I (2) *is/am* looking at (3) *this/these* pandas. (4) *They're/Their* from China.
Ella: Are (5) *they/them* rare?
Pete: Yes. There (6) *isn't/aren't* many pandas in the wild now.
Ella: Look at (7) *that/those* koala. It (8) *is/are* eating leaves. I think it's hungry. Give (9) *it/it's* a sandwich.
Pete: No! You (10) *must/mustn't* feed the animals.
Ella: OK. I'm sorry. Are there (11) *some/any* birds in this park?
Pete: Yes. There is (12) *a/an* eagle (13) *next/next to* the llamas.
Ella: Oh, yes, I can see it. It's fantastic. It's opening (14) *its/it's* wings. Look at (15) *they/them*. They're huge.

☐ 15

TOTAL: ☐ 35

11 Memories

21 GRAMMAR

was/were

1 ★ **Affirmative**
Write the words in the correct order.

1 for/late/I/was/school
   I was late for school.
2 was/It/yesterday/hot
   ....
3 exam/before/were/We/nervous/our
   ....
4 good/video/The/was/very
   ....
5 in/They/asleep/were/the/theatre
   ....
6 for/school/You/late/were/the/bus
   ....

2 ★★ **Affirmative**
Complete the sentences.

At two o'clock yesterday …

1 My brother *was at the cinema* .

2 My friends and I ....

3 My sister ....

4 My grandparents ....

5 My mother ....

3 ★ **Negative**
Complete the sentences with *wasn't* or *weren't*.

1 The food *wasn't* very good.
2 I .... asleep on the sofa.
3 We .... at school on Friday.
4 My grandparents .... at the restaurant.
5 Mike .... nervous about the test.
6 You .... late for school.

4 ★★ **Affirmative and negative**
Write pairs of sentences.

1 Charlie Chaplin/American (✘). He/English (✓).
   Charlie Chaplin wasn't American.
   He was English.
2 Marie Curie/French (✘). She/Polish (✓).
   ....
3 James Dean and Marilyn Monroe/pop stars (✘).
   They/actors (✓).
   ....
4 Salvador Dalí/an architect (✘). He/an artist (✓).
   ....
5 Agatha Christie/an artist (✘). She/a writer (✓).
   ....

Memories 11

VOCABULARY

5 Months
Complete the months and write them in the correct order.

MAY APR SEPT
NOV JUN JAN
FEB MAR AUG
DEC JUL OCT

1 *January*
2 ....
3 ....
4 ....
5 ....
6 ....
7 ....
8 ....
9 ....
10 ....
11 ....
12 ....

Check your answers in the Mini-dictionary.

6 Dates and ordinal numbers
Match the dates (1–6) with the months (a–f). Then write the dates in full.

[5] a) the *thirtieth* of March
[ ] b) the .... of December
[ ] c) the .... of January
[ ] d) the .... of February
[ ] e) the .... of September
[ ] f) the .... of May

7 Look at the picture and correct the information (1–5).

1 It was hot.
   It wasn't hot. It *was cold*.
2 The nurse was early.
   .... She ....
3 The little boy was happy.
   .... He ....
4 The baby was awake.
   .... She ....
5 The man was nervous.
   .... He ....

8 Prepositions
Write the words in the correct list.

June, the tenth of May, seven o'clock, five thirty, the fifth of November, Friday morning, my birthday, Mondays, the second of March, April, September, nine twenty-five, twelve o'clock, February

in	on	at
June	*the tenth of May*	*seven o'clock*
....	....	....
....	....	....
....	....	....
....	....	....

Now complete the rule with *in*, *on* or *at*.

We use .... with months. We use .... with days, days + parts of days, and dates. We use .... with times.

11 Memories

22 GRAMMAR
Questions with *was/were*

1 ★ *Yes/No questions*
Write questions.

1 it/hot/yesterday?
   Was it hot yesterday?
2 I/late/for school?
   ....
3 the play/interesting?
   ....
4 your friends/on holiday/in August?
   ....
5 your teacher/at school/yesterday?
   ....
6 you/at the cinema/yesterday?
   ....

2 ★★ *Yes/No questions and answers*
Complete the questions and write true short answers in your notebook.

1 *Were* you at school at twelve o'clock yesterday?
   Yes, I was. / No, I wasn't.
2 .... your friend at your house yesterday?
3 .... your parents on holiday in June?
4 .... you happy yesterday?
5 .... it cold yesterday?
6 .... you and your friend at the cinema last weekend?

3 ★ *Wh- questions*
Write the words in the correct order. Add capital letters and question marks.

1 at/were/seven/where/you/o'clock
   Where were you at seven o'clock?
2 like/was/the/what/weather/yesterday
   ....
3 cinema/at/you/what time/were/the
   ....
4 with/were/who/you/yesterday
   ....
5 party/was/where/Anna's
   ....
6 teacher's/your/what/was/first/name
   ....

4 ★★ *Wh- questions*
Complete the questions for the answers.

1 *Where were you* at five thirty?
   I was at the cinema.
2 .... in this photo?
   He was six years old.
3 .... yesterday?
   We were at the Internet café.
4 .... the film .... ?
   It was interesting but very long.
5 .... on Friday?
   She was with her friends.
6 .... your favourite film when you were young?
   It was *Star Wars*.

5 ★★ *was/were + Yes/No and Wh- questions*
Tick (✓) the correct questions. Correct the mistakes in the other questions.

1 Were you asleep on the sofa? ✓
2 Where ~~was~~ you in June? *Were*
3 What do the weather like yesterday? ....
4 Were we on holiday on the sixth of May? ....
5 Were the cat asleep in the kitchen? ....
6 Who was you with yesterday? ....

6 ★★ *was/wasn't, were/weren't*
Complete the dialogue.

Tom: What's your first memory?
Rosa: I (1) *was* with my mother and my sister, Katie.
Tom: How old (2) .... you?
Rosa: I (3) .... five.
Tom: Where (4) .... you?
Rosa: We (5) .... on the beach in Spain.
Tom: (6) .... your dad with you?
Rosa: No, he (7) .... He (8) .... in London – at work!
Tom: What (9) .... the weather like?
Rosa: It (10) .... hot and sunny. Katie (11) .... asleep.
Tom: (12) .... you happy?
Rosa: Yes, I (13) .... It (14) .... a lovely day.

VOCABULARY

7 Weather
Match the words (1–8) with the pictures (a–h).

Use your Mini-dictionary to help you.

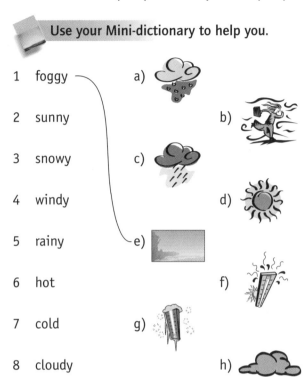

1 foggy
2 sunny
3 snowy
4 windy
5 rainy
6 hot
7 cold
8 cloudy

8 Write the answers to the questions in your notebook.

1 Is it sunny today?

Yes, it is./No, it isn't.

2 What was the weather like yesterday?
3 Is it hot in July in your country?
4 When is it rainy in your country?
5 Is it cold in December in your country?
6 What was the weather like last weekend?

9 Times
Match the times (1–6) and (a–f).

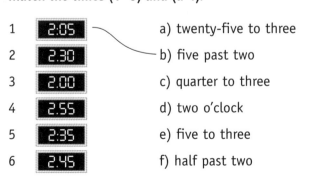

1 2:05   a) twenty-five to three
2 2:30   b) five past two
3 2:00   c) quarter to three
4 2:55   d) two o'clock
5 2:35   e) five to three
6 2:45   f) half past two

10 *past* and *to* for time
Write the times, using *past* and *to*.

Use your Mini-dictionary to help you.

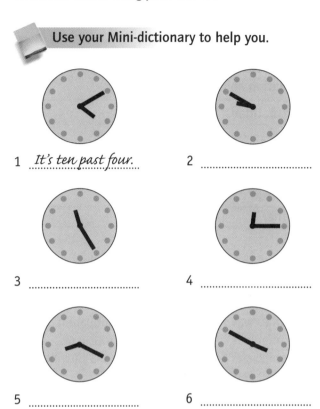

1 *It's ten past four.*
2 ....
3 ....
4 ....
5 ....
6 ....

Word Corner

1 Look at the extract from the Mini-dictionary. Match the words (1–6) to the correct part.

sightseeing /ˈsaɪtˌsiːɪŋ/ *noun* the activity of visiting famous buildings and places when you are on holiday: *Let's go **sightseeing** in the city centre this afternoon.*

1 word   c   4 example
2 pronunciation   5 definition
3 word type   6 stress mark

2 Match the words (1–8) with the pronunciation (a–h).

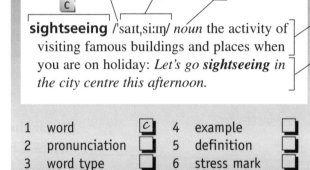

1 eight   a) /ˈlɪsən/
2 Wednesday   b) /ɡɪˈtɑː/
3 friend   c) /raɪt/
4 listen   d) /ˈwenzdi/
5 daughter   e) /ˈdɔːtə/
6 people   f) /frend/
7 guitar   g) /eɪt/
8 write   h) /ˈpiːpəl/

11 Memories

Reading and Writing

1 Reading
Read the text and complete the table with information about Daniel.

First holiday	
Where?	Paris in France
When?	
How old?	
Who with?	
Weather?	

My first holiday – Daniel Fisher, 10. February. 2002

I remember my first holiday very well. It was in Paris in France. I was eight years old. My sister was twelve. We were there with our parents from 31. March to 7. April. The weather was cold. It wasn't rainy. On the first four days we were in the centre of Paris. I wasn't very happy in the galleries and museums – they were boring.

On 4. April it was my birthday. I was awake at 6 a.m. My birthday was great. We were at Disneyland all day. The characters were fantastic. The food was nice.

On 8. April at 9 p.m. we were on the plane for London. My dad was nervous. My mum was relaxed. My sister and I were very happy. It was a fantastic holiday.

2 Read the text again and correct the information in these sentences. Write them in your notebook.

1 Daniel was in Paris with his grandparents.
2 Daniel was boring on the first four days.
3 Daniel was asleep at 6 a.m. on his birthday.
4 Daniel was sad on his birthday.
5 Daniel's parents were nervous on the plane.

3 Punctuation: Dates
Correct the dates in the text.

My first holiday – Daniel Fisher, 10 February 2002

4 Answer these questions with dates in numbers and words in your notebook.

1 What's today's date?

17 March

2 What was yesterday's date?
3 What's the date of your birthday?
4 What's the date of your best friend's birthday?
5 What was the date of your last exam?

5 Write these dates as numbers.

1 the twenty-eighth of June two thousand   28/6/00
2 the fifth of November two thousand and one   ....
3 the first of February nineteen ninety-eight   ....
4 the twenty-second of May two thousand   ....
5 the fourteenth of August two thousand and two   ....
6 the third of January nineteen ninety-seven   ....

6 Linking with *and/but*
Link these sentences with *and* or *but*.

1 I was eight years old. My sister was twelve.
   I was eight years old and my sister was twelve.
2 The weather was cold. It wasn't rainy.
   ....
3 The characters were fantastic. The food was nice.
   ....
4 My dad was nervous. My mum was relaxed.
   ....
5 The beach was nice. The weather was good.
   ....
6 Our coach was late. The trip was interesting.
   ....

Memories 11

CHECK YOUR GRAMMAR AND VOCABULARY

1) was/were
Complete the sentences with *was/were* or *wasn't/weren't*. (1 mark each)

1. I .... at the cinema yesterday.
2. My friends .... on the beach last weekend.
3. My mother .... at home at one o'clock. She was at work.
4. .... you and your friends late for school? No, we ....

[5]

2) Write questions with *was/were*. (1 mark each)

1. where/the children/at five o'clock?
   ....
2. you/at school/this morning?
   ....
3. when/she/in London?
   ....
4. what time/Dave/at the sports centre?
   ....
5. what/weather/like/yesterday?
   ....

[5]

3) Ordinal numbers
Write the numbers as ordinals. (0.5 marks each)

Example: **5** – *fifth*

1. **1** – ....
2. **3** – ....
3. **8** – ....
4. **14** – ....
5. **22** – ....
6. **30** – ....

[3]

4) Opposites
Write the opposites of these adjectives. (0.5 marks each)

1. asleep ....
2. cold ....
3. relaxed ....
4. happy ....
5. late ....
6. bad ....

[3]

5) Weather
Write adjectives under the pictures. (0.5 marks each)

1. ....
2. ....
3. ....
4. ....

[2]

6) Prepositions
Complete the sentences with the correct preposition: *in*, *on* or *at*. (0.5 marks each)

1. I go swimming .... Mondays.
2. Is your birthday .... April?
3. The film started .... half past seven.
4. We played tennis .... Friday morning.

[2]

Check your progress

Circle the correct word. (1 mark each)

Alice: My favourite house (1) *was/were* our (2) *once/first* house.
Sonia: What (3) *does/was* it like?
Alice: Not very big, but it (4) *wasn't/was* lovely.
Sonia: Where was (5) *the/a* house?
Alice: It was (6) *near/next* the beach. (7) *In/On* July and August, my friends and I (8) *was/were* on the beach every weekend.
Sonia: (9) *Who/How* old (10) *was/were* you?
Alice: I (11) *was/were* fifteen.

Sonia: Where is your new house?
Alice: In the town centre. There (12) *is/are* nice shops and cafés but I (13) *not/don't* go to (14) *they/them* very often.
Sonia: Where do you like (15) *going/go*?
Alice: To the beach – it's lovely and quiet there.

[15]

TOTAL: [35]

12 At night

23 GRAMMAR

was/were and time expressions

1 ★ *yesterday* or *last*?
Write the words in the correct list.

morning, year, evening, night, week, afternoon, month, Sunday, weekend

yesterday	last
morning	*year*
....	....
....	....
	....
	....
	....

2 ★ *was/were* + time expressions
Write the words in the correct order. Add capital letters and full stops (.).

1 last/on/were/we/holiday/month
   We were on holiday last month.
2 morning/school/were/they/at/yesterday
   ....
3 yesterday/town/in/was/she/the/centre/afternoon
   ....
4 last/were/in/you/Italy/month
   ....
5 the/were/the/students/in/library/yesterday
   ....
6 last/at/my/was/grandmother/home/night
   ....

3 ★ *wasn't/weren't* + time expressions
Write negative sentences.

1 He/at home/last night
   He wasn't at home last night.
2 Helen/at the cinema/yesterday afternoon
   ....
3 My parents/at work/last week
   ....
4 I/late for school/yesterday morning
   ....
5 You/in the coffee bar/yesterday
   ....
6 We/on holiday/last month
   ....

4 ★★ *Yes/No* questions and short answers
Write questions and true short answers in your notebook.

1 you/at school/yesterday?

> *Were you at school yesterday?*
> *Yes, I was./No, I wasn't.*

2 your teacher/on holiday/last week?
3 your parents/at home/last night?
4 you and your family/in the same town/last year?
5 your best friend/at your school/last year?
6 you/with your friends/yesterday evening?

5 ★★ *Wh-* questions
Write questions for the answers.

1 *Where were you last night?*
   I was at home last night.
2 ....?
   John was with his parents yesterday.
3 ....?
   My parents were on holiday in June.
4 ....?
   We were with our grandparents last week.
5 ....?
   Fiona was in the coffee bar yesterday morning.
6 ....?
   They were in New York last year.

At night 12

6 ★★ All forms
Complete the dialogue with the correct form of *was/were* or a time expression.

Paula: Is your memory good?
Sam: I don't know really.
Paula: Well, where (1) *were* you (2) *yesterday* morning?
Sam: That's easy. I (3) .... with my friends in town.
Paula: OK. Where (4) .... you and your friends on this day (5) .... year?
Sam: Oh, I'm not sure. I think we (6) .... at school.
Paula: OK. How old (7) .... your mum on her last birthday?
Sam: Forty-two!
Paula: Very good. Now, what (8) .... on TV (9) .... evening?
Sam: I don't know. I (10) .... at home. My friends and I (11) .... at a coffee bar.
Paula: OK. How much (12) .... the drinks and sandwiches?
Sam: My coffee (13) .... £1.50 and my cheese sandwich (14) .... £2.80.
Paula: Your memory is brilliant!

8
What are your favourite places in Exercise 7? (number 1 = your favourite).

9 Prepositions
Complete the second sentence with *before* or *after*.

1 I have a shower. Then I have breakfast.
 = I have a shower *before* breakfast.
2 They do their homework. Then they have dinner.
 = They do their homework .... dinner.
3 She has dinner. Then she sees her friends.
 = She sees her friends .... dinner.
4 You do your homework. Then you go to school.
 = You do your homework .... school.
5 We have lunch. Then we play tennis.
 = We play tennis .... lunch.

10
In your notebook, write five true sentences about what you do on school days. Use the words in the box.

before school, before lunch, after school, before dinner, after dinner

VOCABULARY

7 Places
Match the objects (1–8) with the places (a–h).

a) cinema
b) bowling alley
c) fast-food restaurant
d) concert
e) library
f) Internet café
g) coffee bar
h) amusement arcade

12 At night

24 GRAMMAR
there was/there were and *there wasn't/there weren't*

1 ★ Affirmative
Look at the list of activities at the city festival last week. Write sentences.

City festival!
- a disco
- football matches
- a rock concert
- a street party
- art classes
- rare animals
- fast food
- children's games

1 *There was a disco.*
2 *There were some football matches.*
3 ....
4 ....
5 ....
6 ....
7 ....
8 ....

2 ★ Negative
The things in the box weren't at the city festival last week. Write negative sentences with *a* or *any*.

classical concert, films, pop stars, photographer, play, film stars, bowling alley

1 *There wasn't a classical concert.*
2 *There weren't any films.*
3 ....
4 ....
5 ....
6 ....
7 ....

3 ★★ Affirmative and negative
Write sentences.

1 a disco (✓)/a concert (✗)
   There was a disco but there wasn't a concert.
2 sandwiches (✓)/pizzas (✗)
   There were some sandwiches but there weren't any pizzas.
3 a coffee bar (✓)/a restaurant (✗)
   ....
4 photos (✓)/paintings (✗)
   ....
5 library (✓)/sports centre (✗)
   ....
6 lions (✓)/tigers (✗)
   ....

4 ★★ Questions and short answers
Look at the list in Exercise 1. Write questions and short answers about the city festival.

1 a disco
   Was there a disco?
   Yes, there was.
2 pop stars
   Were there any pop stars?
   No, there weren't.
3 a street party
   .... ?
   ....
4 art classes
   .... ?
   ....
5 a classical concert
   .... ?
   ....
6 film stars
   .... ?
   ....

5 ★★ *was/were*, *there was/there were*
Complete the dialogue.

Sally: (1) *Were* you at the festival last week?
Clara: Yes, I (2) ....
Sally: What (3) .... it like?
Clara: Great! There (4) .... lots of people and the weather (5) .... good.
Sally: (6) .... there any pop stars?
Clara: No, there (7) .... , but there (8) .... a fantastic rock concert. And there (9) .... a street party on the last night. All my friends (10) .... there. Where (11) .... you?
Sally: We (12) .... at home. We (13) .... on holiday in Spain. It (14) .... great.

At night 12

6 ★★★ *was/were, there was/there were*
In your notebook, write sentences about these things.

- the last festival in your town/city
- your last holiday
- your last party
- your last trip

The last festival in my town wasn't very good. There wasn't any pop music.

VOCABULARY

7 TV programmes
Complete the TV guide with the words in the box.

news, soap, film, sports programme, game show, documentary, cartoon, comedy

BBC 1
6.00 Today (1) *News* and weather from around the world.
7.00 Win! Win! Win! Big money prizes in this new (2) ....

BBC 2
6.00 Mickey and Donald A classic Disney (3) ....
7.00 Animal habitat (4) .... on the rare European bison.

8 Put the dialogue in the correct order. Number the boxes.

[1] **Andy:** What was on TV last night? I was out.
[ ] **Bella:** *Fun Festival*.
[ ] **Andy:** Was it good?
[ ] **Bella:** Don't worry. I've got the match on video for you.
[ ] **Andy:** Was there a football match on?
[ ] **Bella:** Yes, it was very interesting. And after the documentary, there was an American comedy, but it wasn't very funny.
[ ] **Andy:** What was it called?
[ ] **Bella:** No, but there was a great tennis match. Pete Sampras was the winner.
[ ] **Andy:** Oh, I really like him.
[ ] **Bella:** There was a documentary on life in Africa.

9 Circle the adjectives in the box that can describe TV programmes.

interesting, angry, boring, large, exciting, funny, sunny, great

ITV
6.00 Life and love 175th episode of this American (5) ....
7.00 The Bob Banks Show Very funny (6) ....

CHANNEL 4
6.00 Team time US (7) .... with American football and basketball.
7.00 (8) .... : *Texas Star* Black and white western.

Word Corner

Look at the underlined words and circle the correct meaning, a, b or c.

1. There is a big <u>community</u> of Chinese people in my city. A lot of them have got restaurants.
   a) town   b) family   **c) group**
2. There are fast cars on this road. <u>Pedestrians</u> mustn't walk in the road.
   a) people in cars   b) people on foot   c) people in buses
3. Your clothes, books and CDs are on the floor. You must <u>tidy</u> your bedroom.
   a) invite your friends to   b) clean   c) put things on shelves and in cupboards
4. You must <u>revise</u> before the next exams. Your results were bad last time.
   a) study things from your lessons again   b) do your homework   c) write

Check your answers in the Mini-dictionary.

12 At night

Reading and Writing

1 Reading
Look at the TV guide quickly and find the answers.

1 What time is Disneytime on?
   ....
2 Which programmes are new?
   ....
3 What time are the tennis matches on?
   ....
4 What types of film are on?
   ....

Saturday 8 April
BBC 1
5.05 **News, Weather.**
5.30 **Disneytime** Favourite cartoons.
6.00 **Star For A Night** Music show with people who want to be a star.
7.00 **Smith And Jones** New comedy show.
8.00 **FILM: Men In Black** Science fiction comedy starring Will Smith.
9.50 **Match Of The Day** Today's football matches.

BBC 2
4.30 **Tennis** Davies Cup matches – Britain and Portugal.
6.00 **Team Play** New game show for teenagers.
6.30 **Science Now** Documentary on science in schools.
7.30 **FILM: Fast!** Action movie.
9.30 **News, Weather.**

2 Read the TV guide more slowly. Are these sentences true (T) or false (F)?

1 The film is on after the sport on BBC1. ☐
2 There isn't a soap on. ☐
3 The news on BBC 2 is on after the news on BBC 1. ☐
4 There is more comedy on BBC 2 than BBC 1. ☐
5 There is a western on. ☐
6 The game show is on before the documentary on BBC 2. ☐

3 Punctuation: Capital letters
Correct these sentences. Write capital letters where necessary.

1 My favourite film is the matrix.
2 Do you like shakespeare's romeo and juliet?
3 A: Who's your favourite actor?
   B: bruce willis.
4 There was a good film on last night – mickey blue eyes.
5 My favourite game show is the alphabet game.

4 A personal e-mail
Are these adjectives positive or negative? Which one isn't positive or negative?

worried, surprised, happy, bored, angry, sad, funny, nervous

positive: ....
negative: ....
not positive or negative: ....

5 Re-write the e-mail message in full sentences in your notebook. Use the key on page 86 of the Students' Book to help you.

Dear Nicola

Thank u 4 your message. I'm very :-). It was my birthday yesterday and there was a party. I was very 8□o. I've got a new video – it's very :-D!

R u OK? Don't be <:-o about your exams. U r a good student. My girlfriend is :-(. Her piano exam was very difficult yesterday, but her teacher isn't >-(.

I must do my homework b4 t. Say hi 2 your mum and dad.

C u soon

Lol

Adam

Dear Nicola,
Thank you for your message.

At night 12

CHECK YOUR GRAMMAR AND VOCABULARY

1 *was/were, wasn't/weren't* + time expressions
Complete the sentences. (1 mark each)

1 I was on holiday .... week.
2 Were they at home .... afternoon?
3 We .... with our friends yesterday.
4 I .... at school yesterday. It was a holiday.
5 The weather .... sunny yesterday.

[5]

2 *there was/were*
Write affirmative/negative sentences or questions. (1 mark each)

+ = affirmative   − = negative   ? = question

1 there/a jazz concert (−)
   ....
2 there/a street party (?)
   ....
3 there/some messages (+)
   ....
4 there/any tourists (−)
   ....
5 there/any new students (?)
   ....

[5]

3 Word groups
Write the words in the correct list. (0.5 marks each)

angry, breakfast, library, funny, documentary, coffee bar, tea, soap, fast-food restaurant, dinner, game show, amusement arcade, worried, cartoon, surprised, Internet café

Meals	Places	Adjectives	TV programmes
....	....	....	....
....	....	....	....
....	....	....	....
	....	....	....
	....		

[8]

4 Prepositions
Complete the second sentence with *before* or *after*. (0.5 marks each)

1 I have a shower. Then I clean my teeth.
   I clean my teeth .... my shower.
2 I read a book. Then I go to bed.
   I read a book .... bedtime.
3 I feed my dog. Then I have breakfast.
   I feed my dog .... breakfast.
4 I have my aerobics class. Then I have a shower.
   I have a shower .... my aerobics class.

[2]

Check your progress

Circle the correct word. (1 mark each)

Harry: Where (1) *was/were* you
(2) *yesterday/last* night? You
(3) *weren't/wasn't* at football practice.
Alex: I (4) *was/am* out with my parents.
(5) *Were/Was* there a lot of people at the football?
Harry: No, there (6) *weren't/wasn't* and the teacher (7) *was/were* angry.
Alex: Sorry. What was on TV (8) *afternoon/after* the practice?
Harry: There (9) *was/were* a good western and a funny comedy show.
Alex: Oh, I (10) *not/don't* like westerns much.
(11) *Was/Were* there a football match on?
Harry: Yes, there (12) *was/wasn't* – Manchester United and Leeds.
Alex: Great! (13) *Have/Do* you got (14) *a/an* video of the match?
Harry: Yes. Come and watch (15) *it/him* later.
Alex: OK, thanks.

[15]

TOTAL: [35]

73

13 Accidents

25 GRAMMAR
Past Simple affirmative

1 ★ **Regular verbs**
Complete the sentences with the verbs in the box.

ask, play, rain, watch, cook, arrive

1 The teacher _asked_ us some difficult questions.
2 We .... a great video last night.
3 She .... late for the party.
4 The weather was very bad yesterday. It .... all day.
5 You .... tennis very well.
6 I .... dinner for my parents.

2 ★★ **Regular verbs**
Complete the text with the verbs in brackets.

Last Saturday was a bad day. I wanted to play football, but it (1) _rained_ (rain). I (2) .... (stay) at home and (3) .... (watch) my favourite basketball team on TV. They weren't very good! In the evening, there was an accident near our house with a car driver and a girl on a bicycle. The driver (4) .... (stop) and my mum (5) .... (phone) for an ambulance. The ambulance (6) .... (arrive) in five minutes and then the police (7) .... (arrive), too. The police (8) .... (ask) the driver some questions. The girl (9) .... (stay) in hospital for three days but she's OK now. Her bicycle helmet (10) .... (save) her.

3 ★ **Regular and irregular verbs**
Write the verbs in the correct part of the table. Then write the irregular verbs in the Past Simple.

turn, have, leave, play, watch, go, stay, put, cook, ask, see, phone, save, make, fall, take, give, wake, arrive, rain

Regular	Irregular →	Irregular Past Simple
turn	have →	had
....	.... →	....
....	.... →	....
....	.... →	....
....	.... →	....
....	.... →	....
....	.... →	....
....	.... →	....
....	.... →	....
....	.... →	....
....	.... →	....

4 ★★ **Irregular verbs**
Write sentences in the Past Simple. Add capital letters and full stops (.).

1 I/have lunch/at one o'clock
 I had lunch at one o'clock.
2 we/leave school/at four thirty
 ....
3 my parents/go/to town/by taxi
 ....
4 she/see/her friends/last night
 ....
5 my mother/take/my friend/home
 ....
6 the doctor/give/me some medicine
 ....
7 my brother/fall off/his bicycle
 ....

Accidents 13

5 ★★ Regular and irregular verbs
Complete the text with the verbs in brackets.

Yesterday was Friday and my friend, Gina, (1) _stayed_ (stay) the night at our house. After dinner, we were in my bedroom. I (2) .... (have) some new posters and Gina (3) .... (ask), 'Why aren't they on the walls?' Gina (4) .... (get up) on the chair and (5) .... (put) one poster on the wall. Then she (6) .... (turn) and (7) .... (fall off) the chair. She (8) .... (hit) her head on the cupboard. My parents were out and I was very worried. I (9) .... (phone) the ambulance and Gina's parents. They all (10) .... (arrive) in five minutes. The ambulance (11) .... (take) Gina to hospital and her parents (12) .... (go), too. Gina (13) .... (wake up) in hospital and she was very surprised. The nurses (14) .... (give) her some medicine. I (15) .... (see) her this morning and she wasn't angry with me. I'm very lucky!

6 ★★ Regular and irregular verbs
Tick (✓) the correct sentences and correct the mistakes in the other sentences.

1 I went to school by bus last Monday. ✓
2 We ~~stay~~ at home last night. _stayed_
3 She fall off her bicycle yesterday. ....
4 The police asked me some questions after the accident. ....
5 He wake up late yesterday morning. ....
6 We phoned our friends yesterday. ....
7 You leave at 7.30 a.m. yesterday. ....
8 My friend and I have a party last week. ....

VOCABULARY

7 Words that go together
Circle the word/words that go with the verbs.

arrive	(early), (late), to school, your house
turn	a corner, a question, a game
ask	a question, for help, to the teacher, an answer
fall off	a chair, the floor, a bicycle
leave	the house, school, from a room, at 8.30 a.m.
wake up	well, in the morning, late
put on	your clothes, a hat, some shoes, an umbrella
give	a present, a party, some medicine, a question
hit	a person, a car, an accident
save	a person, a helmet

8 Accidents, fire and crime
Look at the pictures and write the jobs (1–5).

Use your Mini-dictionary.

1 _fire fighter_
2 ....
3 ....
4 ....
5 ....

9 Put the words in the correct list.

fire brigade, police station, hospital, police, ambulance, fire engine

Group   Place
fire brigade   ....
....

Transport
....
....

13 Accidents

26 GRAMMAR
Past Simple affirmative and negative

1 ★ Negative
Write negative sentences.

1 I got up early yesterday.
   I didn't get up early yesterday.
2 The driver stopped after the accident.
   ....
3 You arrived late.
   ....
4 She put on her helmet.
   ....
5 We left the house at seven thirty.
   ....
6 He phoned his girlfriend last night.
   ....
7 I saw my grandparents last weekend.
   ....
8 The survey showed new results.
   ....

2 ★ Affirmative and negative
These people did a motorbike test. Write sentences about the results.

	put on a helmet	stop at the junction	see the pedestrian	turn corners fast
Angela	✗	✓	✗	✓
Mike	✓	✓	✓	✗
Kim	✓	✗	✗	✗
Richard	✗	✗	✓	✓

1 Mike/stop at the junction
   Mike stopped at the junction.
2 Angela/put on a helmet.
   Angela didn't put on a helmet.
3 Mike and Richard/see the pedestrian
   ....
4 Mike and Kim/turn corners fast
   ....
5 Kim and Richard/stop at the junction
   ....
6 Angela/turn corners fast
   ....
7 Angela and Mike/stop at the junction
   ....
8 Kim/see the pedestrian
   ....

3 ★ Affirmative and negative
Look at the picture. Write sentences about what Dave did and didn't do in his bedroom yesterday. Use the verbs in the box.

play the guitar, watch TV, wear jeans, have breakfast, play computer games, have a Coke

1 *Dave played the guitar.*
2 *He didn't watch TV.*
3 ....
4 ....
5 ....
6 ....

4 ★★ Affirmative and negative
In your notebook, write true sentences about what you did and didn't do yesterday.

5 ★★ Affirmative and negative
Complete the text with the verbs in brackets. Use the Past Simple.

I (1) *had* (have) a bicycle accident when I was thirteen. I (2) .... (take) risks in those days. For example, I (3) .... (not wear) a helmet and I (4) .... (not stop) at junctions. One Sunday morning, I (5) .... (go) to my friend's house by bicycle. I was late and I (6) .... (have to) go fast. After ten minutes, I (7) .... (turn) right but I (8) .... (not look) first. I (9) .... (not see) a motorcyclist and he (10) .... (hit) me. We both (11) .... (fall off) our bikes. I was unconscious but the motorcyclist was OK. He (12) .... (phone) for an ambulance and I (13) .... (wake up) in hospital. I wear my helmet now and I don't take risks.

Accidents 13

VOCABULARY

6 Road safety
Look at the picture. Complete the sentences with the words in the box.

cyclist, zebra crossing, seat belt, motorcyclist, junction, driver, helmet, pedestrian

1 The *cyclist* isn't wearing a ....
2 The car .... is wearing a ....
3 The .... is walking on the ....
4 The .... is near the police car.
5 The cyclist is near the ....

Look at the picture again. Who is taking a risk?

....

7 In your notebook, copy and complete the word map with the words in the box.

pedestrian, van, helmet, bicycle, junction, seat belt, corner, cyclist, car, protect, driver, motorbike, zebra crossing, lorry, motorcyclist

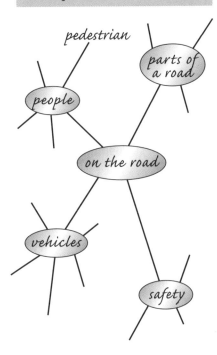

8 Prepositions
Complete the sentence with the correct preposition, a, b or c.

1 I woke *up* in hospital after the accident.
   a) on   b) off   c) up
2 Put .... your jumper. It's cold.
   a) to   b) on   c) off
3 They phoned .... an ambulance.
   a) for   b) at   c) to
4 He went to school .... taxi.
   a) by   b) in   c) on
5 Watch .... ! That car isn't stopping.
   a) in   b) out   c) off
6 You must stop .... the junction.
   a) to   b) at   c) in

Word Corner

Look at the underlined words and circle the correct meaning. Read the sentences carefully to help you.

1 I can't study at home. My brothers and sisters are very noisy.
   a) not quiet   b) tired   c) intelligent
2 The theatre was full but it wasn't very good and the audience was bored.
   a) people who watch a football match
   b) people who watch a play or show
   c) actors and actresses
3 Sorry I'm late. I came by car and the traffic was very bad.
   a) road   b) cars, buses, lorries   c) weather
4 I like my town in summer. The weather is good and we have a festival.
   a) a part of the year   b) an activity   c) a city
5 Our team didn't win and we were very disappointed.
   a) happy   b) excited   c) sad

77

13 Accidents

Reading and Writing

1) Reading
Put the pictures in the correct order.
Then read the story and check your answer.

1 ☐ 2 ☐ 3 ☐ 4 ☐

I saw an accident in town yesterday. there was a woman in the street near the zebra crossing My mum stopped our car at the zebra crossing and then the woman walked into the road. There was a motorcyclist but he didnt see the woman and he didn't stop I shouted, 'Watch out!' The motorcyclist hit the woman and then he fell off his motorbike. I had my mobile phone and I called for an ambulance The motorcyclist got up and my mum asked, 'Are you OK' The woman didnt get up – she was unconscious and the motorcyclist was worried. The ambulance arrived in five minutes and then the police arrived, too. the ambulance driver took the woman to hospital. the police asked the motorcyclist my mum and me some questions

2) Read the story again. Are these sentences true (T) or false (F)?
1 The girl and her mother had an accident yesterday. ☐
2 The motorcyclist crashes into the woman. ☐
3 The girl's mother called for an ambulance. ☐
4 The motorcyclist was unconscious after the accident. ☐
5 The motorcyclist didn't go to the hospital. ☐

3) Linking with *and then*
Look at this example of *and then* from the story. Underline the other examples in the story.

My mum stopped our car at the zebra crossing and then the woman walked into the road.

4) Now write these sentences with *and then* in your notebook.
1 last Sunday I got up late/had a big breakfast

Last sunday I got up late and then I had a big breakfast.

2 I went swimming/saw my friends
3 we went to the amusement arcade/went to the coffee bar
4 we had some sandwiches/had some cake
5 we went to my house at 5 p.m./watched a video
6 my friends went home at 7 p.m./I did my homework

5) Punctuation: Review
Correct the text. Add capital letters, full stops (.), apostrophes ('), commas (,) and question marks (?) where necessary.

There was a woman in the street near the zebra crossing.

6) Spelling
Correct these spelling mistakes.
1 hospitall — *hospital*
2 polise — ....
3 teatre — ....
4 tenis — ....
5 futball — ....
6 vidio — ....
7 telefone — ....
8 casette — ....

Accidents 13

CHECK YOUR GRAMMAR AND VOCABULARY

1 Past Simple
Complete the sentences with the verbs in brackets. Use the Past Simple. (1 mark each)

1. The cyclist .... (not wear) a helmet.
2. I .... (leave) home at 7 p.m. yesterday evening.
3. He .... (not stop) at the junction.
4. My friends and I .... (see) an accident last night.
5. The driver .... (turn) the corner fast.
6. The survey .... (not show) any interesting results.
7. The accident .... (happen) in the town centre.
8. It .... (not rain) last week.
9. The lorry .... (hit) the car at the junction.
10. My mum .... (take) us to school by car.

[10]

2 Accidents and road safety
Circle the correct word. (0.5 marks each)

1. The ambulance *fighter/driver* took the boy to hospital.
2. There's a fire! Phone the fire *brigade/office*.
3. The fire *lorry/engine* arrived in five minutes.
4. The police *fighter/officer* asked us some questions.
5. The nurses gave Adam some *medicine/doctor*.
6. You must stop at a zebra *junction/crossing*.
7. Wear your *drive/seat* belt in the car.
8. *Cyclists/Pedestrians* mustn't walk in the road.
9. Don't *take/make* risks on the road.
10. A helmet *saves/protects* your head.

[5]

3 Verbs and prepositions
Complete the sentences with the words in the box. (1 mark each)

| up, off, on, up, out |

1. Watch .... ! There's a dog in the road.
2. The boy didn't put .... his helmet.
3. I woke .... early yesterday morning.
4. The motorcyclist fell .... his bike.
5. We didn't get .... at 7.30 a.m.

[5]

Check your progress

Circle the correct word. (1 mark each)

Lisa: There (1) *is/was* an accident (2) *near/next* our school yesterday.
Ross: Really? I didn't (3) *see/saw* it.
Lisa: A man in (4) *a/an* car (5) *hits/hit* a girl. She was on (6) *his/her* bike and she (7) *fell/fall* off. She (8) *don't/didn't* have a helmet.
Ross: That's very silly. You must (9) *wear/wore* a helmet on your bike. (10) *Were/Was* the girl OK?
Lisa: I don't know. A teacher phoned (11) *to/for* an ambulance (12) *before/after* the accident. (13) *An/The* ambulance arrived very quickly and (14) *took/take* the girl to hospital.
Ross: And the car driver?
Lisa: He (15) *were/was* OK.

[15]

TOTAL: [35]

14 Missing home

27 GRAMMAR
Comparative adjectives: one and two syllables

1 ★ Comparative forms
Complete the sentences with the comparative form of the adjectives in the box.

fast, old, hard, big, friendly, cold

1 We've got a new car. It's *faster* than our old car.
2 I like my new teacher. She's .... than my old teacher.
3 Put on your jumper. It's .... today than yesterday.
4 I'm worried. That test was .... than our last test.
5 I'm fifteen but my sister is .... than me.
6 Our new flat is very small. Our old flat was ....

2 ★ Comparatives with *to be*
Write sentences. Use the correct form of *to be*. Add capital letters and full stops (.).

1 London/big/Oxford
  London is bigger than Oxford.
2 Turkey/hot/England
  ....
3 my brothers/old/me
  ....
4 the weather today/bad/the weather yesterday
  ....
5 those computers/small/these computers
  ....
6 my team/good/your team
  ....
7 motorbikes/noisy/cars
  ....

3 ★ Comparing people
Look at the adjectives.

tall   short   heavy   light   slow   fast

Now correct the information about John and David. Write the sentences in your notebook.

JOHN WALKER
17 years 2 months
1.8 metres
70 kilos
two sisters and a brother
brilliant at maths
can run 100 m in 12 seconds

DAVID COOPER
17 years 6 months
1.75 metres
65 kilos
three brothers and a sister
good at maths
can run 100 m in 10 seconds

1 David is younger than John.
  David is older than John.
2 John is shorter than David.
3 John is lighter than David.
4 David's family is smaller than John's family.
5 John is worse at maths than David.
6 David is slower than John.

Missing home 14

4 ★★ **Comparatives with to be**
Write sentences that are true for you. Write the sentences in your notebook. Use the correct form of *to be*.

1 I/old/my best friend

> I'm older than my best friend./
> I'm younger than my best friend.

2 English/easy/maths
3 this week/cold/last week
4 rock groups/good/heavy metal groups
5 I/small/my mum
6 my friends/noisy/me

VOCABULARY

5 **Word groups**
Add three words to each group.

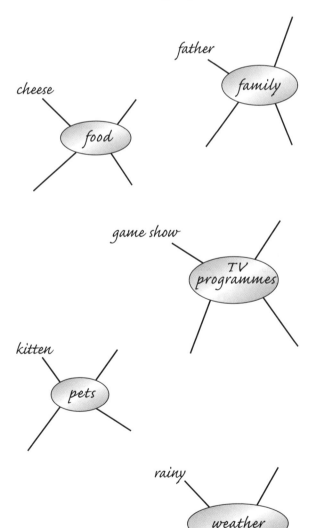

6 **Adjectives**
Match the sentences (1–6) with the reasons (a–f).

1 I miss the food from home. [c]
2 We miss the TV programmes.
3 He misses his home town.
4 They miss the people.
5 She misses the trains.
6 I miss the weather.

a) It's smaller than London.
b) They're friendlier than in England.
c) It's better than in England.
d) They're faster than in England.
e) It's sunnier than in England.
f) They're better than in England.

7 Complete the crossword with the opposites of clues 1-7.

Across
1 small
4 unfriendly
6 cold
7 hard

Down
2 bad
3 quiet
5 early

8 **Prepositions**
Circle the correct word.

1 We go on holiday *in*/*at* August.
2 I was at home *in*/*at* seven thirty.
3 We go swimming *in*/*at* summer.
4 Her birthday is *in*/*at* June.
5 We went shopping *in*/*at* the weekend.
6 I get up *in*/*at* seven o'clock.

14 Missing home

28 GRAMMAR
Comparative adjectives: two and three syllables

1 ★ Comparative forms
Complete the sentences with the comparative form of the adjectives in the box.

expensive, nervous, exciting, serious, difficult

1 Those jeans are cheap. Your jeans were _more expensive_ .
2 Today's homework was easy. Yesterday's was ....
3 His last book was funny. His new book is ....
4 My friend was relaxed before the exam, but I was ....
5 The first film was boring, but the second was ....

2 ★ Comparatives with *to be*
Write sentences with the comparative form of the adjectives. Use the correct form of *to be*.

1 my picture/colourful/your picture
My picture is more colourful than your picture.
2 art galleries/interesting/churches
....
3 rock music/exciting/classical music
....
4 my sister/intelligent/my brother
....
5 your story/realistic/my story
....

3 ★★ Comparative forms
Look at the information about the cafés. Complete the sentences, using the adjectives in the box.

big, near, expensive, friendly, good, colourful, quiet

1 Blueline is _bigger_ than Joe's.
2 The coffee at Joe's is .... than at Blueline.
3 The sandwiches at Blueline are .... than at Joe's.
4 Blueline is .... than Joe's because they don't play music.
5 The walls are .... at Blueline than at Joe's.
6 Joe's is .... to school than Blueline.
7 The waiters are .... at Joe's than at Blueline.

Which coffee bar do you prefer?

4 ★★ Comparative forms
Complete the text with the correct form of the adjectives in brackets.

Dear Sam,

We're in London now and it's great. It's (1) _bigger_ (big) than my home town and much (2) .... (exciting). It's got lots of modern galleries and museums. I think they're (3) .... (interesting) than the historic places. The weather today is much (4) .... (good) than yesterday when it rained. There is a festival and the streets are (5) .... (colourful) than they usually are.

There are one or two problems, too! The food is (6) .... (bad) than at home and everything is (7) .... (expensive). The shops close (8) .... (early) here than at home, too!

Lots of love,

Ana

JOE'S CAFÉ
- 10 tables
- fantastic coffee
- sandwiches – £2.(
- good music
- black and white walls
- 10 minutes from school
- very friendly waiters

BLUELINE CAFÉ
- 20 tables
- good coffee
- sandwiches – £3.00
- no music
- red and blue walls
- 20 minutes from school
- unfriendly waiters

5 ★★★ Comparing cities

In your notebook, write sentences comparing two cities in your country. Use the adjectives in the box.

expensive, exciting, small, colourful, friendly, cold

The capital city is more expensive than my city.

VOCABULARY

6 Seasons, months and weather

Look at the seasons column. Write the letters in the correct order. Then complete the table with information for your country.

Seasons	Months	Weather
isrnpg – spring		
eumsmr –		
nuuatm –		
tiwrne –		

7 Likes and dislikes

Match the questions (1–5) and answers (a–e).

1. What's your favourite season? **c**
2. What do you do in summer?
3. What is your town like in winter?
4. When is your town busy?
5. Do you like winter?

a) No. I don't like cold weather.
b) In summer. There are lots of tourists then.
c) My favourite season is spring.
d) It's very quiet.
e) I go to the beach with my friends.

8 Write true answers to these questions in your notebook.

1. What's your favourite season?
2. Why do you like it?
3. What do you do in that season?
4. What is your town like in that season?

Word Corner

1 Look at the dictionary extract for *go*.
Match the words (1–8) to the correct part (a–h).

go (gəʊ) (verb)
present: I/you/we/they **go**, he/she/it **goes**;
past: I/you/he/she/it/we/they **went**
am/is/are **going**
1 to move or travel towards a place
Let's **go** to the cinema
Does this bus **go** to the stadium?

1 word	a	5 -ing forms	
2 definition		6 past form	
3 word type		7 pronunciation	
4 example		8 present forms	

2 Write these verb forms.

1. -ing form of *run*: .running....
2. past of *run*: ....
3. he/she/it form of *do*: ....
4. past of *give*: ....
5. -ing form of *hit*: ....
6. he/she/it form of *have*: ....
7. past of *fall*: ....
8. -ing form of *swim*: ....

Check your answers in the Mini-dictionary.

14 Missing home

Reading and Writing

1) Postcard layout
Write the numbers on the correct part of the postcard.

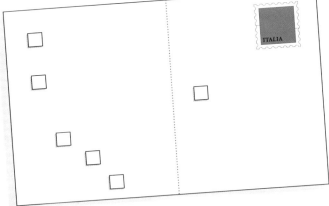

1 Write soon!

2 I arrived in Rome last weekend. I'm staying with a very nice family and I'm practising my Italian. Everything is OK but I miss you very much. Yesterday was our first day at the language school. We had lessons in the morning. Then we went on a trip. I was very happy because we saw some beautiful places. The weather here is hot and sunny – better than in England!

 5 Kate

 3 Dear Mum and Dad,

6 Mr and Mrs pr johnson
72 new street
oxford
UK

 4 Lots of love,

2) Read the postcard in the correct order and circle the correct information.

1 Kate is *English/Italian*.
2 Kate misses *Italy/her parents*.
3 Kate is a *student/teacher* at a language school.
4 Kate went *shopping/sightseeing* in Rome.
5 The weather is *hotter/colder* in Italy than in England.

3) Punctuation: Titles and addresses
Write the title and address with the correct punctuation. Add capital letters where necessary.

....
....
....
....

4) Linking with *because, and, but, then*
Match the lines in columns A and B. Look at the linking words (in **bold**) and match the meanings (a–d) to the sentences 1–4.

A	B	
1 I'm staying with a very nice family	**Then** we went on a trip.	a) a reason
2 Everything is OK	**because** we saw some beautiful places.	b) sequence of actions
3 We had lessons in the morning.	**and** I'm practising my Italian.	c) contrast
4 I was very happy	**but** I miss you very much.	d) more information

5) Choose the correct word.

1 I'm tired *because/then* I got up very early.
2 We went shopping. *But/Then* we had lunch.
3 I like summer *but/and* I don't like winter.
4 I did my homework at nine o'clock. *Then/Because* I went to bed.
5 Why are you late? *Because/But* the bus didn't arrive.
6 The party was good *but/and* the food wasn't very nice.

CHECK YOUR GRAMMAR AND VOCABULARY

1 Comparatives
Complete the sentences with the correct form of the adjectives in brackets. (1 mark each)

1. The maths results were .... (bad) than the science results.
2. My friend was .... (nervous) about the exams than me.
3. I think British TV is .... (serious) than American TV.
4. I think English is .... (easy) than German.
5. You are .... (intelligent) than me.
6. Books are .... (expensive) than CDs.
7. This summer is .... (hot) than last summer.
8. You are .... (good) at art than I am.
9. Skiing is .... (exciting) than swimming.
10. My bedroom is .... (big) than my brother's bedroom.

[10]

2 Word groups
Circle the odd one out. (0.5 marks each)

1. autumn, spring, summer, weather
2. water, spaghetti, sandwich, cake
3. soap, game show, news, video
4. rainy, noisy, snowy, windy

[2]

3 Opposites
Write the opposites. (0.5 marks each)

big	small
cold	....
....	late
friendly	....
funny	....
....	difficult
bad	....
....	expensive
boring	....

[4]

4 Prepositions
Complete the sentences with *at* or *in*. (1 mark each)

1. We went skiing .... winter.
2. I had lunch .... one thirty.
3. We don't go to school .... August.
4. Do you go swimming .... the weekend?

[4]

Check your progress

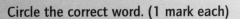

Circle the correct word. (1 mark each)

Sue: Where (1) *am/are* you from?
Ana: I'm from Spain but I (2) *live/lived* in London now.
Sue: (3) *Do/Are* you miss Spain?
Ana: I (4) *am miss/miss* my family and my home town in spring.
Sue: Why?
Ana: There (5) *is/are* a festival every year in April.
Sue: Did you (6) *went/go* to (7) *a/the* festival last year?
Ana: Yes, I did. It (8) *is/was* fantastic. There (9) *was/were* hundreds of people in the streets, and food, music, and dancing.
Sue: What (10) *was/did* the weather like?
Ana: Sunny and hot. The weather in Spain is usually (11) *good/better* than in England.
Sue: How often do you (12) *go/going* to Spain?
Ana: (13) *Twice/Two* a year.
Sue: You speak English very (14) *good/well*.
Ana: You must learn Spanish. It's very (15) *easy/easier*!

[15]

TOTAL: [35]

29 GRAMMAR
going to for future plans

1 ★ Affirmative
Complete the sentences with the full forms of *going to* and the verb in brackets.

1 I *am going to see* (see) my friends tomorrow.
2 She .... (do) her homework later.
3 My friends .... (have) a party this weekend.
4 We .... (visit) our grandparents this afternoon.
5 You .... (study) for the exams.
6 John .... (play) football tomorrow.

2 ★★ Affirmative
Complete the diary days with your plans for next week. Then write five sentences in your notebook. Use short forms.

Monday *football 5 p.m.,* ....
Tuesday ....
Wednesday ....
Thursday ....
Friday ....

I'm going to play football on Monday afternoon.

3 ★ Negative
Write negative sentences. Use short forms.

1 We/not/play tennis/tomorrow
   We aren't going to play tennis tomorrow.
2 I/not/use my computer/this evening
   ....
3 You/not/come/to the party
   ....
4 She/not/wear/her new dress
   ....
5 They/not/get up/early/tomorrow
   ....
6 My teacher/not/give us a test/next week
   ....

4 ★★ Affirmative and negative
Write pairs of sentences. Use short forms.

1 the children – play football
   The children aren't going to play football.
   They're going to play tennis.

2 the motorcyclist – put on his hat
   ....
   ....

3 the girl and her boyfriend – see a concert
   ....
   ....

4 the businesswoman – use her mobile phone
   ....
   ....

5 ★ Yes/No questions

Write questions and short answers.

1 you/study for the exam? (yes)
   Are you going to study for the exam?
   Yes, I am.
2 he/come to the party? (no)
   .... ?
   ....
3 they/stay in tonight? (yes)
   .... ?
   ....
4 it/rain at the weekend? (no)
   .... ?
   ....
5 Ana/watch TV tonight? (yes)
   .... ?
   ....
6 you/phone your friend later? (no)
   .... ?
   ....

6 ★★ Wh- questions and answers

Write questions and true answers in your notebook.

1 what/you/do tonight?

What are you going to do tonight?
I'm going to play computer games.

2 what/you/do next weekend?
3 when/you/study for the exams?
4 what time/you/get up tomorrow?
5 when/your teacher/give you a test?
6 what/your parents/do next weekend?

VOCABULARY

7 Exams and revision

Circle the correct word.

1 Where do you *revise*/*revision*?
2 We're going to *make*/*do* an exam next week.
3 *Make*/*Do* some physical exercise when you revise.
4 It's a good idea to make a revision *timetable*/*worktable*.
5 Work with your friends and *test*/*exam* their knowledge.
6 Physical exercise is *relaxing*/*relax* when you do exams.

8 Look at the list of tips about exams. Put them in order. (1 = best)

TIPS
- start my revision early ☐
- plan my revision ☐
- revise with my friends ☐
- make notes of things I don't understand ☐
- go to bed early before an exam ☐
- eat breakfast before an exam ☐
- surf the Internet to revise ☐
- revise for short periods and then stop ☐

In your notebook, write a plan for your next exams. Use your top five tips from the list.

I'm going to start my revision early.

9 Prepositions : Review

Complete the sentences with the prepositions in the box. You can use them more than once.

at, in, on, to, next to, after, near, before

Time
1 I get up ..*at*.. half past seven.
2 We're going to buy a new computer .... Saturday.
3 I don't watch TV .... the afternoon.
4 She doesn't like going out .... night.
5 I always have a shower .... I go to bed.
6 We get the results a week .... the test.

Place
7 Is there a video .... the classroom?
8 Put these books .... the shelf, please.
9 I sit .... my friend in class.
10 My school is very .... my house. It's only five minutes on foot.

Movement
11 You mustn't arrive late .... the party.
12 They went .... London last month.

30 GRAMMAR
have/has to, don't/doesn't have to

1 ★ have/has to
Complete the sentences with *have/has to* and the verbs in the box.

study, do, wear, go, stay, write

1 We *have to study* for the English test.
2 My sister had an accident yesterday. She .... in hospital for a week.
3 My parents work at weekends and I .... the shopping.
4 James .... to bed early before exams.
5 You .... a letter to your grandparents.
6 I .... a uniform at school.

2 ★ don't/doesn't have to
Circle the correct form.

1 I *doesn't*/*don't* have to go to school today.
2 You *doesn't*/*don't* have to answer all the questions.
3 He *doesn't*/*don't* have to leave early.
4 We *doesn't*/*don't* have to walk to school.
5 My friends *doesn't*/*don't* have to do the test.
6 Diana *doesn't*/*don't* have to work today.

3 ★★ Affirmative and negative
Read the messages and write sentences.

1 Sally and Chris/do their homework
   Sally and Chris have to do their homework.
2 Chris/clean the kitchen
   Chris doesn't have to clean the kitchen.
3 Sally/buy a newspaper
   ....
4 Chris and Sally/make lunch
   ....
5 Chris/clean his football boots
   ....
6 Chris and Sally/feed their pets
   ....
7 Sally/write a letter
   ....
8 Chris/phone his dad
   ....

4 ★ Yes/No questions
Write questions.

1 we/go to bed early
   Do we have to go to bed early?
2 I/do my homework now
   .... ?
3 she/wear a uniform at school
   .... ?
4 you/wear a helmet on your bike
   .... ?
5 Mike/work at weekends
   .... ?
6 they/answer questions about pop music
   .... ?

Dear Sally

We're at the hospital with grandpa. Please remember to

feed the dog
buy a newspaper
clean the kitchen
do your homework

See you later.

Love

Mum and Dad

Dear Chris

I'm at the supermarket. Please remember to

phone your dad
do your homework
clean your football boots
feed the cat

See you at 2 p.m.

Love

Mum

Tests 15

5 ★ Wh- questions
Complete the questions with *have to* and the verbs in brackets.

1 Where *does* the driver *have to go*? (go)
2 What time .... we .... ? (get up)
3 How long .... my composition .... ? (be)
4 What .... she .... in the game show? (do)
5 Where .... I .... ? (sit)
6 What .... the children .... ? (wear)
7 How often .... you .... (do) exams?

6 ★★★ All forms
Complete the dialogue with the correct form of *has/have to*.

Teacher: We're going on a trip tomorrow.
Alice: (1) *Do we have to* leave early?
Teacher: Yes, we do. We (2) .... leave at seven thirty.
Tom: And (3) .... we .... wear our uniform?
Teacher: No, you (4) ....
Alice: Great! What clothes (5) .... we .... wear?
Teacher: You (6) .... wear jeans, a jumper and trainers. We are going to be in the countryside.
Sara: (7) .... I .... bring sandwiches from home?
Teacher: Good question. Yes, all students (8) .... bring sandwiches and a drink from home. And bring pens and your notebooks because you (9) .... do a project on the area.
Tom: How long (10) .... the project .... be?
Teacher: About four pages.

Word Corner

Choose the correct word.

1 Are you going to stay (in)/off tonight?
2 It's raining. Put your boots *on/off*.
3 What time do you get *down/up* in the morning?
4 I was nervous and I woke *up/off* three times last night.
5 I hit my head when I fell *down/off* a chair.
6 Do we have to write *after/down* the answers.

Check your answers in the Mini-dictionary.

VOCABULARY

7 Helping at home
Match the pictures with the words in the box.

tidy your room, feed the dog, wash the dishes, clean the car, take the dog for a walk, tidy the garden

1 *tidy your room*

2 ....

3 ....

4 ....

5 ....   6 ....

8 Feelings
Complete the sentences with the adjectives in the box.

bored, excited, nervous, disappointed, relaxed

1 The new game show wasn't very interesting. We were *bored* when we watched it.
2 We were very .... when we didn't win the big prize.
3 My mum was on a TV game show. I was very .... when I saw her.
4 I was very worried before the exam, but now I'm more ....
5 'Don't be .... ,' the presenter said. 'The questions are very easy.'

15 Tests

Reading and Writing

1) Reading
Read and answer the questions in the quiz.

Test your general knowledge!

1. Whats the capital of Greece?
2. Which is bigger, Argentina or Italy?
3. How many states are there in the USA – 49, 50 or 25?
4. Wheres Tower Bridge? – New York, London or Paris?
5. Who is David Beckhams wife?
6. Whats the name of Madonnas daughter?
7. Was Charlie Chaplin English or American?
8. What was the name of U2s first CD?
9. Who was Picasso?
10. Was Marie Curie French, Polish or Russian?
11. How many times did Martina Navratilova win Wimbledon?
12. Was Pelé a footballer, a tennis player or an athlete?
13. Whats the eighth month of the year?
14. Whens American Independence Day?
15. How many days are there in February?

2) Punctuation: Apostrophes
Correct the quiz. Write apostrophes where necessary.

> 1 What's the capital of Greece?

3) Now correct these sentences. Write apostrophes where necessary.

1. You dont have to answer all the questions.
2. Im going to watch *Who wants to be a Millionaire?*
3. She isnt going to revise this evening.
4. Are you going to clean the car? No, Im not.
5. My friend doesnt tidy her room.
6. The presenters name is Johnny Star.

4) Punctuation: Commas
Correct these sentences. Write commas (,) where necessary.

1. I like game shows films and cartoons.
2. He has to clean the car feed the cat and tidy his room.
3. We're going to finish our project have dinner and then watch TV.
4. You have to read a text answer some questions and then write a composition.
5. Do we have to do a listening speaking or writing test?
6. I planned my revision revised every day and got good results.

5) Spelling
Correct the spelling mistakes in these words.

1. revize — *revise*
2. frendly
3. earlyer
4. hoter
5. autum
6. colourfull
7. nowledge
8. strenth
9. fysical
10. milionaire

CHECK YOUR GRAMMAR AND VOCABULARY

1 going to
Complete the sentences with short forms of *going to* and the verbs in brackets. (1 mark each)

1 I .... (finish) my homework.
2 .... you .... (watch) the football match?
3 He .... (visit) his penfriend this summer.
4 My parents .... (buy) a new car.
5 It's very cold. .... it .... (snow) later?

[5]

2 have/has to
Complete the sentences with the correct form of *have/has to*. (1 mark each)

1 We .... go to school tomorrow because it's a holiday.
2 .... they .... work this evening? Yes, they ....
3 .... she .... study every day?
4 You must do exercises 1 and 2 but you .... do the other exercises.

[5]

3 Exams and revision
Complete the sentences with the verbs in the box. (1 mark each)

test, do, revise, make, do

1 It's important to .... before exams.
2 How often do you .... exams?
3 .... a revision timetable before you start.
4 These exams .... general knowledge.
5 .... some physical exercise when you revise.

[5]

4 Helping at home
Choose the correct word. (0.5 marks each)

1 I *look at/after* my brother when my parents go out.
2 Do you have to *wash/clean* the dishes?
3 Remember to *take/make* the dog for a walk.
4 We have to *wash/tidy* our room once a week.
5 In my house my dad *cleans/tidies* the car.
6 I *help/go* my parents with the shopping.

[3]

5 Prepositions review
Correct the underlined prepositions. (0.5 marks each)

1 I don't work in Saturdays. ....
2 We play basketball on weekends. ....
3 Our next test is at the 24th May. ....
4 I have a shower after I leave home. ....

[2]

Check your progress

Circle the correct word.

Dear Richard,

I'm (1) **write/writing** this letter (2) **in/at** my bedroom. I'm not very happy because (3) **it rains/it's raining** and we have exams soon. I (4) **have/has** to revise every day and it's boring! What do you (5) **doing/do** when you have exams? Have you got (6) **some/any** tips for me?

After the exams, I (7) **going to/am going** to relax. My family and I (8) **are/is** going to visit my grandparents in the United States (9) **in/on** August. I miss (10) **him/them**, because we don't (11) **go/going** to the United States very often.

What (12) **do/are** you going to do (13) **at/in** the summer? You (14) **must to/must** visit (15) **us/we** here in Rome soon.

It's revision time again!

Best wishes

Daniele

[15]

TOTAL: [35]

16 Goodbye

31 GRAMMAR
Suggestions

1 ★ *Let's ...*
Write suggestions for the situations. Use the verbs and the nouns from the box.

verbs: go, watch, have, find, paint, go

nouns: swimming, a party, the walls, a teacher, a video, home

2 ★ *Why don't/doesn't ...?*
Write the words in the correct order. Add capital letters and question marks.

1 the/he/why/doesn't/see/doctor
   Why doesn't he see the doctor?
2 go/why/we/don't/fishing
   ....
3 teacher/they/don't/the/why/ask
   ....
4 you/don't/help/why/I
   ....
5 the/she/doesn't/why/surf/Internet
   ....
6 down/don't/why/you/sit/
   ....

3 ★★ *Why don't ...?* and *Let's ...*
Complete the dialogues with *Why don't/doesn't* + pronoun, or *Let's*.

1 A: I'm hungry.
   B: *Why don't you* make a sandwich?
2 A: It's our teacher's last day at school today.
   B: .... buy her a cake to say 'Thank you'.
3 A: He doesn't understand his homework.
   B: .... ask his teacher for help?
4 A: This is a lovely park.
   B: .... take a photo of it.
5 A: We can't play tennis – it's cold and rainy.
   B: .... play on an indoor court.
6 A: They want information for their project.
   B: .... surf the Internet?

92

Goodbye 16

4 ★★ Why don't ...? and Let's ...
In your notebook, write the dialogue in complete sentences. Add capital letters, question marks (?) and full stops (.) where necessary.

Alan: let/go out/tonight
Bob: OK. where/you/want/go
Alan: why/we/not/go/Internet café
Bob: it/not open/today
Alan: OK. let/play/tennis
Bob: Good idea. what time/you/want/to play
Alan: at half past seven. why/you/not/have dinner/at our house
Bob: OK, thank you

> *Alan: Let's go out tonight.*

5 ★★★ Why don't ...? and Let's ...
Write your suggestions for these situations in your notebook.

1 Your parents want to go out.

> *Why don't you go to a restaurant?*

2 It's your best friend's birthday.
3 Your friend is nervous before an exam.
4 Your grandparents want to go on holiday.
5 Your father wants to learn English.

VOCABULARY

6 Complete the sentences about the people in the picture. Use the words in the box.

wave, hug, cry, smile, kiss goodbye, shake hands

1 The boy _is waving_ .
2 The tourists _____ .
3 The businesswomen _____ .
4 The old lady _____ .
5 The husband and wife _____ .
6 The girl _____ .

7 Complete the dialogues with the words in the box.

Goodbye (x2), Bye (x2), meet, See, Give, too

Formal
Mr Jones: (1) _Goodbye_ .
Dr Brown: (2) _____ . It was nice to (3) _____ you.
Mr Jones: Yes, you (4) _____ .

Informal
Simon: (5) _____ , Emma.
Emma: (6) _____ , Simon. (7) _____ me a call.
Simon: OK. (8) _____ you.

8 Prepositions
Choose the correct word.

1 Do you live *at*/*in* a big house?
2 Were you *at*/*in* the festival last month?
3 Don't stay *in*/*at* bed very late.
4 My parents are *in*/*at* the United States.
5 Let's have a party *in*/*at* home.
6 The children are playing *in*/*at* the street.

16 Goodbye

32 GRAMMAR
Verb forms: Review

1 ★ **All verb forms**
Choose the correct verb form.

1 **Write** to me soon.
   (Imperative)/Present Simple
2 **I'm** not nervous.
   to be: present/past
3 **He's playing** the guitar.
   Present Simple/Present Continuous
4 We **weren't** at home at 5 p.m.
   to be: present/past
5 I **get up** late at weekends.
   Present Simple/Present Continuous

2 ★ ***to be* (Present Simple)**
Complete the sentences with the correct form of *be*.

1 I *am* Polish.
2 Where .... they from?
3 He .... a singer. He's an actor.
4 .... you hungry? No, I ....
5 Mum and Dad .... at home. They're at the cinema.
6 You .... late. You're early.

3 ★★ **Imperatives and *have/has got***
Write sentences in your notebook.

1 go/bookshop/great books
   Go to that bookshop. It's got great books.
2 eat in/café/horrible food
   Don't eat in that café. It's got horrible food.
3 go/gallery/fantastic paintings
4 visit/wildlife park/boring animals
5 take photos in/the city centre/lovely places
6 go/Internet café/old computers

4 ★ **Present Simple (affirmative and negative)**
Complete the sentences with the correct form of the verbs in brackets.

1 I *get up* (get up) early every day.
2 She .... (watch) TV in the evening.
3 My brother .... (go) to school on foot.
4 He .... (not live) near me.
5 My friend .... (not study) German.
6 I .... (not like) dogs very much.

5 ★ **Present Simple questions**
Write questions in your notebook.

1 you/go/to bed/at eleven o'clock?
   Do you go to bed at eleven o'clock?
2 where/he/live?
   Where does he live?
3 they/like/westerns?
4 James/play football/or basketball?
5 what/you/wear/at school?
6 how often/your parents/go/to the theatre?
7 where/you and your friends/play basketball?

6 ★ **Present Continuous**
Write questions and answers in your notebook.

1 she/study? – yes
   Is she studying? Yes, she is.
2 what/they/do? – they/play football
   What are they doing? They're playing football.
3 you/do/your homework? – no
4 where/your brother/go? – he/go/to school
5 they/make/lunch? – yes
6 Helen/listen/to music? – no
7 who/he/phone? – he/phone/his penfriend

7 ★★ **Present Simple or Continuous?**
Choose the correct verb.

1 I (get up)/am getting up at 7 a.m. every day.
2 What *are you doing/do you do* at the moment?
3 They *use/are using* the computer at the moment.
4 *Do you like/Are you like* swimming?
5 Listen! The teacher *is talking/talks*.
6 How often *is he going/does he go* on holiday?

8 ★★ ***was/were***
Write the sentences and questions in the past in your notebook. Add a time expression.

1 They are at the cinema.
   They were at the cinema yesterday.
2 What is the weather like?
   What was the weather like on Monday?
3 I'm in the garden with my friends.
4 We aren't hungry.
5 Is he in the town centre?
6 Where are your parents?
7 You aren't late for school.

Goodbye 16

9 ★★ Past Simple
Complete the sentences with the past form of the verbs in brackets. There are regular and irregular verbs.

1 The police _arrived_ (arrive) in five minutes.
2 She .... (wake up) early yesterday.
3 The driver .... (stop) at the zebra crossing.
4 Cars .... (not have) seat belts in 1850.
5 The doctor .... (give) me some medicine.
6 James .... (not put on) his helmet.

10 ★★★ All verb forms
Complete the dialogue with the correct form of the verbs in brackets.

Ann: Hello?
Tina: Hello, it's Tina here. I'm in town.
Ann: What (1) _are_ you _doing_ (do) in town?
Tina: I (2) .... (buy) some new clothes. Do you want to meet me here?
Ann: Well, my sister and I (3) .... (do) our homework at the moment.
Tina: OK. Why don't we go to the cinema this evening? The Matrix is on. (4) .... you .... (like) science fiction films?
Ann: Yes, but I (5) .... (go) to the cinema twice last week. I (6) .... (not want) to go again. Let's go to a disco.
Tina: OK. Where (7) .... you .... (want) to go?
Ann: Well, Star Disco (8) .... (be) boring last Friday. Let's go to Central tonight.
Tina: OK. What time (9) .... it .... (open)?
Ann: At nine o'clock. (10) .... (meet) me at quarter to nine near the clock tower.
Tina: OK. See you tonight.

11 ★★★ All verb forms
Tick (✓) the correct sentences. Correct the mistakes in the other sentences.

1 I use my computer every day. ✓
2 We aren't ~~study~~ at the moment. _studying_
3 They are students from Manchester. ....
4 She likes write letters. ....
5 What time are you have lunch every day? ....
6 I were at work yesterday. ....
7 Not go out. It's raining. ....
8 She take the boy to hospital yesterday. ....
9 Dad is watching TV at the moment. ....
10 Are you a doctor? No, I don't. ....

VOCABULARY

12 Word groups
Circle the odd one out.

1 grandmother   sister   wife   (brother)
2 sofa   TV   cooker   video
3 small   grey   green   pink
4 camera   board   ruler   calculator
5 lunch   food   breakfast   dinner
6 pitch   court   racket   pool
7 plane   coach   tourist   train
8 jeans   skirt   T-shirt   wear
9 male   puma   chimp   eagle
10 first   once   third   second

13 Prepositions
Complete the sentences with the prepositions in the box.

to, before, at, by, on (x3), next to, in, after

1 What time do you go _to_ school?
2 My birthday is .... the fifth of May.
3 I do my homework .... the evening.
4 Does he go to work .... bus?
5 You must clean your teeth .... you go to bed.
6 We have English lessons .... 2.30 p.m.
7 We go to school .... foot.
8 We have geography .... Wednesdays.
9 I'm sitting .... my best friend.
10 I don't go swimming in the morning. I go .... school.

16 Goodbye

Reading and Writing

1 Reading
Read the text quickly. Tick (✓) the activities that the text describes.

- cinema
- theatre
- classical music
- dancing
- shopping
- travelling
- eating in a restaurant
- going to an Internet café

1 Is techno your favourite music?
Go to the Party club on New Street to dance to new music from the USA. Open Friday and Saturday, 9 p.m.–2 a.m.

3 Do you like pizza?
Bring your friends to Roma for the best pizza in town. Wonderful food from all parts of Italy. Friendly waiters and good prices. Very busy at weekends so call for a table: 773086.

2 Go surfing!
You don't need a computer at home to surf the Internet. Dotcom has now got ten new computers – and they're very fast. Write e-mails, meet new friends and surf all day. Open 7 days, 8 a.m.–11.30 p.m.

4 Now open! The Film Centre – the citys new arts cinema – is now open. See new films in this fantastic, modern building. Visit the café for great sandwiches, coffees and cakes.
Films:
Mon–Sun at 1.00, 4.00 and 7.00.

2 Read the text again. Are these sentences true (T) or false (F)?

1 The Party club plays American music.
2 The Party club is open every day.
3 Dotcom isn't open at weekends.
4 There are a lot of people at Roma on Saturdays and Sundays.
5 There is a film on three times a day at the Film Centre.

3 Punctuation: Question marks and exclamation marks
Add question marks and exclamation marks to these sentences.

1 Is tennis your favourite sport
2 Do you like travelling
3 Computer lessons start today
4 Football match – don't be late
5 Do you collect CDs

4 Punctuation: Review
Correct these sentences. Add capital letters, full stops (.), apostrophes (') and commas (,).

1 That club plays rap techno and jazz.
2 we're open on mondays, wednesdays and fridays.
3 The new arts centre is fantastic It's open every day
4 Dont forget to visit the towns new gallery.
5 The café has got friendly waiters great food and wonderful coffee.

5 Linking: *and*, *but*, *then* and *because*
Choose the correct word in brackets to link the sentences. Change capital letters where necessary.

1 The film was interesting. The café was nice. (and/but)
   The film was interesting and the café was nice.
2 Find the phone number. Call the restaurant. (because/then)
   ....
3 I want to surf the Internet. I haven't got a computer. (but/because)
   ....
4 I was late for school. I didn't get up on time. (because/then)
   ....
5 The pizzas are great. They aren't very expensive. (but/and)
   ....
6 They went to the Internet café. They went to the disco. (but/then)
   ....

6 Spelling
Correct the spelling mistakes. Add capital letters where necessary.

1 forteen   *fourteen*   5 fotography ....
2 shelfs   ....   6 sanwich   ....
3 magasine   ....   7 fiveteen   ....
4 swiming   ....   8 umbrela   ....

Goodbye 16

CHECK YOUR GRAMMAR AND VOCABULARY

1 Suggestions
Write these sentences correctly. (1 mark each)

1 Lets go to the cinema.
   ....
2 Why don't he go to the dentist?
   ....
3 Let's to watch a video.
   ....
4 Why we don't have a sandwich?
   ....
5 Let's having a party.
   ....

[5]

2 Verb forms
Complete the sentences with the verbs in brackets. (1 mark each)

1 It's very cold in here. .... (not open) the window.
2 My friends .... (not be) at the sports centre yesterday.
3 Diane .... (go) to school at half past eight.
4 We .... (do) our homework at the moment.
5 I don't understand this word. .... (pass) me the dictionary, please.

[5]

3 Saying goodbye
Match the words with the pictures. (0.5 marks each)

cry ☐   hug ☐   shake hands ☐   wave ☐

[2]

4 Food, drink and music
Write the words in the correct list. (0.5 marks each)

cake, techno, sandwich, crisps, classical, fruit juice, heavy metal, Coke, nuts, salsa

Food and drink   **Music**
....
....
....
....
....

[5]

5 Prepositions
Complete the sentences with *at* or *in*. (0.5 marks each)

1 They're on holiday .... Italy.
2 There's a party .... school on Friday.
3 My parents aren't .... home.
4 There's a big dog .... the street.
5 They live .... a house near the beach.
6 I was .... the theatre yesterday evening.

[3]

Check your progress

Choose the correct word. (1 mark each)

Dear Alison,
I (1) **am/was** at home in Poland now. It's cold here, but it (2) **isn't/don't** raining. What (3) **does/is** the weather like in Cambridge?

My holiday with you (4) **was/were** fantastic. You and (5) **you/your** family were very friendly. I (6) **am liking/like** your parents very much – say thank you to (7) **them/their** from (8) **my/me**. I (9) **has/have** got the photos of (10) **our/we** trip to London. (11) **They're/Their** great.

Why (12) **not/don't** you come to Toruń this summer? There are great places to visit and there is (13) **a/an** new sports centre in town. What (14) **do/does** you think about the idea? Talk to your mum and dad about (15) **it/its**.

Write soon!

Best wishes
Maria

[15]

TOTAL: [35]

97

Paola Rossi

Colour the four flags. Add the information.

Paola is from .... in ....

Mauricio (40) = Pia (38)

Paola (16)   Cristina (.......)   Susana (.......)

FAMILY
- Her father is a scientist.
- Her mother is a ....
- She has got .... sisters.

MUSIC
- She likes .... music.
- She plays the ....
- She doesn't like .... music.

PETS
- She has got a ....
- Its name is ....

SPORT → Her favourite sport is ....

ON PAGE ...

12 Paola meets Mrs ....
20 She talks to .... and ....
30 She writes about her ideal ....
35 She talks to .... and .... about going out.
40 She talks to .... about ....
104 She and .... talk about the class ....
111 She talks to .... at the party.

Adam Nowak

Adam is from .... in ....

Tomasz (.......) = Anna (.......)

Mirek (.......)   Adam (.......)

FAMILY
- His father is an ....
- His mother is a ....
- His brother is a .... at .... in ....

Complete the boxes:

	Adam likes ✓	Adam doesn't like ✗	Adam doesn't say ?
athletics	☐	football ☐	hockey ☐
art	☐	English ☐	science ☐
classical music	☐	heavy metal ☐	techno ☐

ON PAGE ...

10 Adam writes to ....
14 He describes his ....
36 He buys twenty ....
40 He talks to .... about ....
54 He asks Gabriela to go to the ....
64 He shows some .... to the students.
90 He falls off his .... and goes to the ....

98

Profiles

Kostas Dimitriou

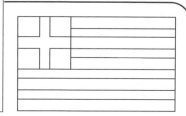

Kostas is from .... in ....

Nikos (40) = Katerina (......)

Kostas (......)   Maria (......)   Eleni (10)

FAMILY
- His mother is a ....
- His father is a ....
- He has got .... sisters.

 photography

 ....

INTERESTS

 ....

 ....

ON PAGE ...

16   Kostas writes about his ....
24   He describes his ....
36   He buys a .... and a book of ....
42   He talks to .... They decide to play ....
70   He talks about the Imperial .... at the Wildlife ....
84   He remembers the trip to ....
111 He dances with .... at the party.

Gabriela Fernandez

Gabriela is from .... in Argentina.

Ricardo (47) = Graciela (45)

Claudia (19)   Gabriela (16)

FAMILY
- Her mother is a teacher.
- Her father is a lawyer.
- Her sister is at ....

STARS
- Her favourite film star is ....
- Her favourite sports star is ....
- Her favourite pop star is ....

PETS
- She has got two ....
- They are called .... and ....

LIKES

....
....
....

DOESN'T LIKE → getting up ....

ON PAGE ...

12   Gabriela meets Mrs ....
20   She talks to .... and ....
22   She writes to her penfriend, ...
56   She goes to the .... with ....
62   She goes sightseeing in ....
78   She talks to .... about first ....
111 She dances with .... at the party.

99

Dictionary quiz

 Use your Mini-dictionary to help you.

1 Look at your Mini-dictionary. Write the correct picture page numbers.

 Shopping – pages ....

Clothes – page ....

 Sports – pages ....

Time – page ....

 Places – pages ....

2 Write these words in alphabetical order. Then write the correct page numbers from the A–Z section.

rainy, home, airport, eighteen, travel, eight, guidebook, popular, zoo, nice

airport – page ....
.... – page ....
.... – page ....
.... – page ....
.... – page ....
.... – page ....
.... – page ....
.... – page ....
.... – page ....
zoo – page ....

3 Add three words to each group. Then check your answers on the picture pages.

4 Match the underlined words (1–7) to the types of words (a–g).

1 That's a lovely painting. ☑ g
2 I wasn't nervous before the exam. ☐
3 It's Mum's birthday. Let's buy her a present. ☐
4 I like football but I don't like tennis. ☐
5 My first school was near my house. ☐
6 You play brilliantly. ☐
7 Are there animals in these forests? ☐

a) linking word e) noun
b) verb f) pronoun
c) preposition g) adjective
d) adverb

5 Match the words (1–6) to the pronunciation (a–f).

1 business a) /ˈkʌbəd/
2 elephant b) /ˈkwestʃn/
3 juice c) /ˈbɪznɪs/
4 cupboard d) /ˈsaɪtˌsiːɪŋ/
5 question e) /dʒuːs/
6 sightseeing f) /ˈelɪfənt/

6 Write the plurals of these nouns.

1 businessman *businessmen*
2 child ....
3 tooth ....
4 foot ....
5 wife ....
6 wolf ....
7 sheep ....

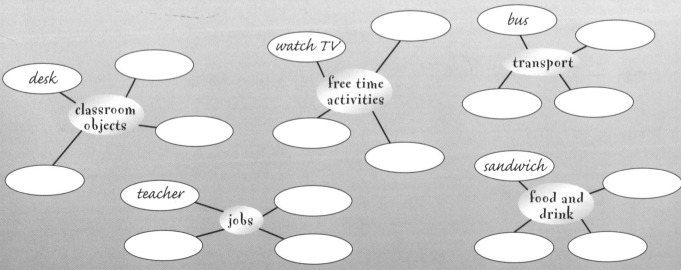

Key Word Bank

1 Hello

Adjectives: great

Asking for personal information: Where are you from? What's your name? Who's your favourite (music/film star)?

Classroom language: learn about, listen to, read dialogues, talk about, write sentences, What's ... in English? What's ... in Polish?

Countries: Argentina, Australia, Britain, Canada, Germany, Greece, Italy, Poland, Russia, Spain, Turkey, the United States

E-mail messages: penfriend, write soon

Meeting people: Hi! My name's ... Hello, my name's... I'm from ...

Music: heavy metal, soul

Nationalities: American, Argentinian, Australian, British, Canadian, German, Greek, Italian, Polish, Russian, Spanish, Turkish

Talking about favourites: my favourite film/sports star/music is...

2 Meet the family

Asking about age: How old are you? I'm fifteen./I'm fifteen years old.

Classroom language: Sorry? Can you repeat that, please?

Families: daughter/son, father/mother, grandfather/grandmother (grandparents), husband/wife, sister/brother, parents/children (kids), surname

Jobs: actor/actress, architect, businessman/woman, computer programmer, doctor, electrician, engineer, housewife, model, scientist, secretary, student, teacher

Numbers: one, two, three, four, five, six, seven, eight, nine, ten, eleven, twelve, thirteen, fourteen, fifteen, sixteen, seventeen, eighteen, nineteen, twenty, twenty-one, twenty-two/-three/-four/-five/-six/-seven/-eight/-nine, thirty, forty, fifty, sixty, seventy, eighty, ninety, one hundred

Prepositions: at, (My brother) is at (university/school/the cinema).

3 At home

Adjectives: bad, big, boring, good, interesting, new, old, small

Animals: cat, dog

At home: bath, bathroom, bed, bedroom, carpet, cooker, door, fridge, garden, kitchen, lamp, (sitting) room, shelf, shower, sofa, table, toilet, wall, window

Colours: black, blue, green, orange, pink, red, white, yellow

Homes: cottage, (block of) flats, house

Home/school objects: book, camera, cassette player, CD player, computer (game), desk, poster, report, television (TV)

On the phone: Give me a call. What's your (home) phone number?

Talking about home: I've got a (small) bedroom. It's got a (big) window and a (red) carpet.

4 At school

Describing things: What's this/that? It's a photo of my brother. What are these/those? They're my favourite CDs.

In the classroom: board, box, chair, clock, cupboard, desk, dictionary, floor, map, paintbrush, pen, poster, ruler, shelf, video

Lessons: art, computer studies, English, geography, history, literature, maths, music, science, sport

Objects: bag, ball, calculator, cassette, computer, dictionary, encyclopaedia, graph, guitar, magazine, map, paintbrush, pen, pencil, photo, piece of paper, rubber, ruler, watch

Plurals: bags, boxes, dictionaries, pens, shelves, watches

5 Going out

Adjectives: beautiful, cheap, expensive, famous, fantastic, historic, terrible

Classroom instructions: ask and answer (the questions), complete (the crossword/table), don't be late (for your lesson), open/close your (books), put your (pencil/pen/books) on the (desk/floor), read (the dialogue on page 40), listen to (the cassette) look at (the photos on page 32), stand up, sit down, work (in pairs/groups), write (a sentence/your name)

Key Word Bank

Expressions: (Three stamps,) please. Here you are. (Brown's is an expensive bookshop.) Don't go there.
Food and drink: (cheese/salad/tomato) sandwich, coffee, orange juice, mineral water, tea
Linking: but
Places: bank, bookshop, café, church, cinema, disco, hotel, main square, market, mosque, museum, newsagent's, park, post office, railway station, statue, restaurant, shop, street, supermarket, town hall
Prepositions: near, (Trinity College) is near (the town centre).
Shopping: CD, envelope, newspaper, postcard, stamp, T-shirt
Sizes: large (L), extra large (XL)
Things to see: films, paintings
Verbs: buy, go to (school/the cinema), take (an umbrella)

6 Playing sport

Abilities: I can speak French. I can't play tennis. Can you swim?
Asking for information: Is there a swimming pool? No there isn't. Are there aerobics classes? Yes, there are.
Asking for permission: Can I open a window, please? Can I go to the toilet, please?
Adverbs: brilliantly, fast, well, very well/not very well
Classes: aerobics, swimming, tennis
Places: basketball court, football pitch, gym, jacuzzi, sauna, sports centre, (indoor/outdoor) swimming pool, tennis court
Sports: athletics, basketball, diving, football, skiing, swimming, tennis
Times: 11.00/eleven o'clock, 06.10/six ten, 11.15/eleven fifteen, 06.20/six twenty, 11.25/eleven twenty-five, 06.30/six thirty, 11.35/eleven thirty-five, 06.40/six forty, 11.45/eleven forty-five, 06.50/six fifty, 11.55/eleven fifty-five
Titles: Mr Jones, Mr S.F. Smith, Ms Edwards, Ms B. Hardy, Mrs Thomas, Mrs J. Brown, Miss James, Miss J.B. Andrews
Verbs: dive, do (the long jump/high jump), jump (three metres), play (basketball/football/tennis), run (the 100 metres in 15 seconds), ski, swim

7 Every day

Activities: dance, play (computer games/the guitar/basketball), travel
Days: Monday, Tuesday, Wednesday, Thursday, Friday, Saturday, Sunday, weekend
Prepositions: at the weekend, on (Fridays), in (the morning/afternoon/evening)
Routines: clean (your teeth), do (your homework/the shopping), get up, go swimming, go (home/to bed/to school/to a disco), have (breakfast/lunch/dinner/a shower), make (breakfast/lunch/dinner) meet (friends/people), read (the newspaper), sleep, study, work

8 Free time

Activities: collect things, go dancing/fishing, go to the cinema, listen to music, play computer games/football/the piano, read books, surf the Internet, take photos, watch videos
Asking about free time activities: Do you play tennis? Yes, I do/No, I don't. What sport do you play? Where do you go swimming? How often do you go dancing?
Films: action film, comedy film, science fiction film, western
Frequency: once a week/month, twice a week/month, three times a week/month, every day/week/month, twice a year
Verbs: like/don't like, love/hate

9 Excursions

Activities: eating (a sandwich), looking at (a map) taking (photos), reading (a book), sightseeing, sitting on (a bus), talking on the phone, walking around (a museum)
Adjectives: ancient, magnificent, modern
Clothes: dress, hat, jacket, jeans, jumper, sandals, shirt, shoes, shorts, skirt, T-shirt, trainers
Places: art gallery, beach, castle, cathedral, cottage, nature reserve, palace, theatre
Prepositions with transport: in a car/taxi, on a bus/train/plane, (We go) to (the city) by (bus/car/train).
Sightseeing: see (buildings/statues), visit collections of paintings/collections of art
Transport: bus, car, coach, plane, train, taxi
Verbs: dance (with a person), kiss, wear (clothes), visit (a place), show (a photo)

10 Wildlife

Adjectives: common, dangerous, friendly, huge, hungry, intelligent, interesting, lovely, rare, small

Animals and birds: bison, camel, chimp, dolphin, elephant, (golden/imperial) eagle, hippo, kangaroo, koala, lion, llama, panda, penguin, puma, rabbit, sheep, tiger, wolf, zebra

Expressions: It's time to ... You mustn't feed the animals.

Parts of the body (animals and birds): ears, eyes, foot (feet), head, legs, neck, wings

Places: Africa, Asia, America (North and South), Australia, Europe, forest, mountains, wildlife park, zoo

Prepositions: near, next to

11 Memories

Adjectives: asleep/awake, cold/hot, happy/sad, late/early, nervous/relaxed

Dates: the nineteenth of February, the second of May

Expressions: Do you remember?

Linking: and, but

Months: January, February, March, April, May, June, July, August, September, October, November, December

Ordinal numbers: first, second, third, fourth, fifth, sixth, seventh, eighth, ninth, tenth, eleventh, twelfth, thirteenth, fourteenth, fifteenth, sixteenth, seventeenth, eighteenth, nineteenth, twentieth, twenty-first, twenty-second ... thirtieth, thirty-first

Prepositions: (My birthday is) on (the twelfth of April). (My exams are) in (July).

Questions (past): What was the weather like? Who were you with? How old were you?

Times: five past/ten past/quarter past/twenty past/twenty-five past/half past (eleven)

past

to

twenty-five to/twenty to/quarter to/ten to/five to (twelve)

Weather: cloudy, foggy, rainy, snowy, sunny, windy

12 At night

Adjectives: angry, bored, funny, happy, nervous, sad, surprised, tired, worried

Expressions: Don't be silly. Guess who (was at the disco.) I was out. You mean ... This is getting (interesting.)

Meals: breakfast (7.30–9.00 a.m.), lunch (12.00 a.m.–1.30 p.m.), tea (4.00–5.00 p.m.), dinner (7.00–8.00 p.m.)

Places: amusement arcade, bowling alley, cinema, coffee bar, concert, fast-food restaurant, Internet café, library, police station, takeaway

Time prepositions: after (six o'clock), before (dinner)

13 Accidents

Adjectives: lucky, quiet, unconscious

Emergency services: ambulance, fire brigade, hospital, police (station)

Emergency vehicles: ambulance, fire engine, police car

Expressions: Watch out! Wear your helmet.

Jobs: ambulance driver, fire fighter, nurse, police officer

Linking: and then

Transport: bicycle/bike, cyclist, driver, helmet, junction, lorry, motorcycle/motorbike, motorcyclist, pedestrian, seat belt, van, zebra crossing

Verbs: arrive (at the party), ask, have (an accident), fall off, give, hit, leave, put on, save, stop, turn, wait (for a bus), wake up

14 Missing home

Adjectives: bad, big, easy, friendly, good, hard, old, small, unfriendly

American/British English: cab/taxi, candy/sweets, cookie/biscuit, elevator/lift, fall/autumn, holiday/vacation, movie/film, shop/store, truck/lorry

Animals at home: pet (cat/dog), owner

Comparatives: better/worse, bigger/smaller, colder/hotter, easier/harder, more boring/colourful/expensive

Expressions: I miss (the food/hot weather). I'm (not) homesick.

Seasons: autumn, spring, summer, winter

Key Word Bank

15 Tests

Adjectives: bored, disappointed, excited, nervous, relaxed, unhappy

Expressions: I have to (clean the car every week). Are you going to (finish your project tonight)?

Nouns for abilities: fitness, intelligence, knowledge, memory, speed, strength

School life: revision, subject, test, timetable, tip (= advice)

Verbs: do (your homework), look after (the children), help (with the shopping), take (the dog for a walk), study (for your exams), tidy (your room), wash (the dishes)

16 Goodbye

Activities: crying, hugging, kissing, shaking hands, smiling, waving

Expressions: Why don't you (write to her)? Let's (watch TV). Thanks for everything. Not at all. Come again.

Food and drink: cake, Coke, crisps, fruit juice, nuts, sandwiches

Linking: then, because

Music: classical, heavy metal, rap, salsa, techno

Mini-Grammar Index

[CAPITALS = main sections of the Mini-Grammar]

a/an **3.1**
any **3.4**

BE (the verb – to be) **1**
be + going to **12.4**

can/can't **8.1**
COMPARATIVES **2**

DETERMINERS **3**
doesn't/don't have to **8.3**

GENITIVE 'S **4**

have/has to **8.3**
HAVE/HAS GOT **5**

IMPERATIVES **6**
-ING FORM **7**

Let's ... **11**

MODAL VERBS **8**
must/mustn't **8.2**

NOUNS **9**

OBJECT PRONOUNS **10**

Past of to be **1.2**
Past Simple **12.3**
POSSESSIVE ADJECTIVES **10**
Present Continuous **12.2**
Present of to be **1.1**
Present Simple **12.1**
Pronouns **10**

SINGULAR AND PLURAL NOUNS **9**
some **3.4**
SUBJECT PRONOUNS **10**
SUGGESTIONS **11**

TENSES **12**
the **3.2**
THERE + BE **13**
there is/are **13.1**
there was/were **13.2**
this/that/these/those **3.3**
Time expressions with the Past Simple **12.3a**

was/were **1.2**
Why don't ...? **11**

Mini-Grammar

1 BE

1.1 Present of *to be*

Uses

Look at the examples of the present of *to be*:
What**'s** your name?
I**'m** English.
He **isn't** a student.
Are you seventeen? Yes, I **am**.
My teachers **are** great.
What**'s** the time? It**'s** seven o'clock.
My name **is** Robert.
Where **are** the boys?
There **are** fifteen students in my class.

Form

+		
I	am ('m)	
He/She/It	is ('s)	English.
You/We/They	are ('re)	

−		
I	am not ('m not)	
He/She/It	is not (isn't)	from Italy.
You/We/They	are not (aren't)	

?		
Am	I	
Is	he/she/it	late?
Are	you/we/they	

Short answers
Yes, I **am**. No, I**'m not**.
Yes, he/she/it **is**. No, he/she/it **isn't**.
Yes, you/we/they **are**. No, you/we/they **aren't**.

1.2 Past of *to be*

Use

We use the past of *to be* to talk about a named time in the past:
We **were** on holiday **last month**.
It **was** cold **last week**.
Who **were** you with **yesterday**?

Form

+		
I/He/She/It	was	at school yesterday.
You/We/They	were	

−		
I/He/She/It	was not (wasn't)	at home last night.
You/We/They	were not (weren't)	

?		
Was	I/he/she/it	late?
Were	you/we/they	

Short answers
Yes, I/he/she/it **was**. No, I/he/she/it **wasn't**.
Yes, you/we/they **were**. No, you/we/they **weren't**.

2 COMPARATIVES

Use

We use a comparative form of an adjective to compare two people or things:
Who is **older** – you or your brother?
He's **older**, but I'm **taller**.
Ana is **younger than** Emily.
CDs are **more expensive than** cassettes.

Form

	adjective	comparative
one syllable	old	old**er**
one syllable ending in -e	nice	nic**er**
one syllable with a short vowel + one consonant	big	big**ger**
two syllables ending in -y	early	earl**ier**
two or more syllables	colourful	**more** colourful

⚡ Some comparatives are irregular:
good – **better**
bad – **worse**
I want to get **better** marks at school next year.
He's **worse** at Maths than me.

⚡ Note that after *than* we use the object pronoun.
She's **older than me**.

3 DETERMINERS

3.1 *a/an*

Uses

We use *a/an* in front of singular countable nouns:
1 to talk about someone's job:
He's **a** doctor and she's **an** engineer.
2 when we mention someone or something for the first time (compare *the*):
We've got **an** old house with **a** big garden.
I can see **a** cat. It's **a** black cat.

Form

- We use *a* in front of nouns and adjectives that start with a consonant:
  a cat, **a** video, **a** blue door
- We use *an* in front of nouns and adjectives that start with a vowel sound (a, e, i, o, u):
  an actress, **an** orange, **an** old man, **an** umbrella

3.2 *the*

We use *the* when the other person knows who or what we are talking about:
The museum is very interesting. (we visited the museum)

*My cat is in **the** garden.* (the garden of my house)

⚡ Compare these sentences:
*Did you go to **a** disco?* (any disco)
*Did you go to **the** disco?* (the disco we usually go to)

3.3 this/that/these/those

Use

We use *this/that/these/those* when we point at something.

- We use *this* (singular) and *these* (plural) for people and things that are near us:
  *Look at **this** picture.* (the picture near me)
  *Do you like **these** jeans?* (I'm wearing/touching the jeans)
- We use *that* (singular) and *those* (plural) for people and things that are not so near us:
  ***That** boy is my friend.* (I'm pointing at the boy)
  ***Those** posters are great.*
  (the posters are on the opposite wall)

Form

- We use *this/that* with singular nouns:
  ***This** music is great.*
  *Where is **that** girl from?*
- We use *these/those* with plural nouns:
  *I like **these** shoes.*
  *Don't touch **those** animals.*

3.4 some/any

We use *some* and *any* in front of plural and uncountable nouns. We usually use *some* in affirmative sentences:
*We've got **some** nice cakes.*
*Please buy **some** cheese.*

- We usually use *any* in questions and negative sentences:
  *Have you got **any** stamps?* (BUT *Do you want **some** tea?*)
  *There aren't **any** discos in this town.*

4 GENITIVE 'S

Uses

1 We use *'s* at the end of a noun to show possession:
John's bike (the bike belongs to John)
the teacher's book (the book belongs to the teacher)

2 We also use *'s* with other meanings. For example:
Jane's brother (the brother of Jane)
the dog's ball (the ball is for the dog)
Sally's eyes (the eyes of Sally)

Form

- We add *'s* to all singular nouns, and plural nouns that don't end in *-s* (e.g. men, women, children):
  the boy's house, Chris's birthday,
  the children's park
- We add an apostrophe (') to plural nouns that end in *-s*:
  my parents' bedroom, her friends' school

⚡ Compare:
the student's books (= the books of one student)
the students' books (= the books of more than one student)

5 HAVE/HAS GOT

Uses

We use *have/has got*:
1 to talk about a person's family:
***She's got** two brothers.*
***Have** you **got** a sister?*
***I've got** a young brother.*
2 to talk about possessions:
***I've got** a new computer.*
***He hasn't got** a CD player.*
3 in descriptions of people/things to talk about their appearance:
***I've got** blue eyes.*
***It's got** long legs.*

Form

+	I/You/We/They He/She/It	have got ('ve got) has got ('s got)	a garden.
–	I/You/We/They He/She/It	have not got (haven't got) has not got (hasn't got)	a computer.
?	Have Has	I/you/we/they got he/she/it	a piano?

Short answers
Yes, I/you/we/they **have**. No, I/you/we/they **haven't**.
Yes, he/she/it **has**. No, he/she/it **hasn't**.

Mini-Grammar

6 IMPERATIVES

- We use the infinitive without *to* for affirmative commands:

  Open *the window!* **Stop!** **Hurry up!**
  Pass *me that dictionary, please.*

- We use *don't* + infinitive without *to* for negative commands:

  Don't touch *the dog!*
  Don't be *nervous!* **Don't worry!**

7 -ING FORM

Use

We use the *-ing* form of the verb like a noun after certain verbs:

She **loves reading**.
I **hate swimming**.
Do you **like learning** English?

Form

- Most verbs add *-ing*:
  watch – watch**ing**, see – see**ing**
- Verbs ending in one *-e*, take off the *-e* and add *-ing*:
  dance – danc**ing**, take – tak**ing**
- Verbs with one syllable ending in one vowel and one consonant, double the consonant and add *-ing*:
  run – run**ning**, swim – swim**ming**
- Verbs ending in *-y*, *-w*, add *-ing*:
  play – play**ing**, grow – grow**ing**

8 MODAL VERBS

8.1 can/can't

Uses

We use *can* + infinitive without *to*:
1 to talk about ability:
I **can ski**.
She **can run** fast.
We **can't play** the guitar.
2 in requests:
Can I **use** your dictionary, please?
Can I **open** the window, please?

Form

+	I/You/He/She/It/We/They	can swim.
−	I/You/He/She/It/We/They	cannot (can't) swim.
?	Can I/you/he/she/it/we/they	swim?

Short answers
Yes, I/you/he/she/it/we/they **can**.
No, I/you/he/she/it/we/they **can't**.

8.2 must/mustn't

Uses

1 We use *must* + infinitive without *to* to say that it is necessary and important to do something:
I **must revise** for my exams.
You **must go** to bed now.

2 We use *mustn't* + infinitive without *to* to tell someone that it is important not to do something:
You **mustn't feed** the animals.
We **mustn't be** late.

Form

+	I/You/He/She/It/We/They	must go.
−	I/You/He/She/It/We/They	must not (mustn't) go.

8.3 have/has to

Use

We use *have/has to* + infinitive without *to* to say that something is necessary:
I **have to tidy** my room. (my mother says I must)
Do we **have to cook** lunch today?

We use *don't have/doesn't have to* + infinitive without *to* to say that something is not necessary.
She **doesn't have to go to** school today.

Form

+	I/You/We/They He/She/It	have to has to	go out.
−	I/You/We/They He/She/It	don't have to doesn't have to	be quiet.
?	Do Does	I/you/we/they he/she/it	have to	go?

Short answers
Yes, I/you/we/they **do**. No, I/you/we/they **don't**.
Yes, he/she/it **does**. No, he/she/it **doesn't**.

Mini-Grammar

9 SINGULAR AND PLURAL NOUNS

- Most nouns add -s in the plural:
  phone – phone**s**, pen – pen**s**
- Nouns ending in -ch, -sh, -s, or -x, add -es in the plural:
  watch – watch**es**, paintbrush – paintbrush**es**, bus – bus**es**, box – box**es**
- Nouns ending in a consonant and -y, change -y to -ies:
  city – cit**ies**, dictionary – dictionar**ies**
- Most nouns ending in -f or -fe, change -f/-fe to -ves:
  shelf – shel**ves**, wife – wi**ves**
- Some plural nouns are irregular:

man – **men**	tooth – **teeth**
woman – **women**	foot – **feet**
child – **children**	sheep – **sheep**
person – **people**	fish – **fish**

10 SUBJECT/OBJECT PRONOUNS AND POSSESSIVE ADJECTIVES

Use

- We use subject pronouns:
  1 in front of verbs:
  I use my computer every day.
  2 so we don't have to repeat a noun:
  My sister is a doctor. **She** lives in the USA.
- We use possessive adjectives in front of nouns:
  My father is an engineer.
  Our school is very big.
- We use object pronouns after verbs and after prepositions:
  My brother is at your school. Do you know **him**?
  Those animals are lovely. Look **at them**.

Form

Subject pronouns	Possessive adjectives	Object pronouns
I	my	me
you	your	you
he	his	him
she	her	her
it	its	it
we	our	us
you (plural)	your	you
they	their	them

11 SUGGESTIONS

Use

We use *Why don't ...?* and *Let's ...* to make suggestions:
Why don't we go to a disco? **Let's go** to a disco!
Let's play tennis. **Why don't we play** tennis?

Form

Why	don't doesn't	I/you/we/they he/she	have a party?
	Let's		watch a video.

12 TENSES

12.1 Present Simple

Uses

We use the Present Simple to talk about:

1 things we do regularly (routines and habits):

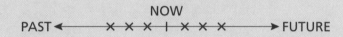

I **go** to school by bus.
I **play** tennis on Saturdays.

2 permanent situations:

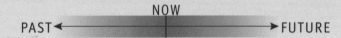

They **live** in Paris.
She **doesn't like** dogs.
He **works** in a bookshop.

3 facts or things that are generally true:
Pumas **live** in forests.
It **snows** in winter in Poland.

Form

+	I/You/We/They He/She/It	work. works.	
–	I/You/We/They He/She/It	do not (don't) does not (doesn't)	work. work.
?	Do Does	I/you/we/they he/she/it	work?

Short answers
Yes, I/you/we/they **do**. No, I/you/we/they **don't**.
Yes, he/she/it **does**. No, he/she/it **doesn't**.

Mini-Grammar

⚡ Rules for the formation of the *he/she/it* forms:
- Most verbs add *-s*:
  live – live**s**
  play – play**s**
- Verbs ending in *-ch*, *-sh*, *-o*, add *-es*:
  watch – watch**es**
  wash – wash**es**
  go – go**es**
  do – do**es**
- Verbs ending in a consonant and *-y*, change *-y* to *-ies*:
  study – stud**ies**
  carry – carr**ies**

12.2 Present Continuous

Use

We use the Present Continuous to talk about activities happening now (at or around the time of speaking):

PAST ←〰〰〰NOW〰〰〰→ FUTURE

*Jane can't go out. She**'s doing** her homework.* (at the time of speaking)
*I**'m learning** Spanish at the moment.* (not at the time of speaking but around this time)

Form

We form the Present Continuous with the present of *to be* + *-ing* form of the verb. See Section 7 for notes on the formation of *-ing*.

+	I He/She/It You/We/They	am ('m) is ('s) are ('re)	working.
–	I He/She/It You/We/They	am not ('m not) is not (isn't) are not (aren't)	working.
?	Am Is Are	I he/she/it you/we/they	working?

Short answers
Yes, I **am**. No, **I'm not**.
Yes, he/she/it **is**. No, he/she/it **isn't**.
Yes, you/we/they are. No, you/we/they **aren't**.

12.3 Past Simple

Use

We use the Past Simple to talk about completed actions and situations in the past:

PAST ←——✕——NOW——→ FUTURE

*I **played** football yesterday.*
*We **went** to Russia last year.*
*She **didn't stop**.*
***Did** you **see** the accident?*

Form

1 For regular verbs, we add *-d* to the infinitive if the verb ends in *e*, and *-ed* if it doesn't end in *e*:
*We **danced** for hours.*
*She **watched** TV last night.*

2 To form questions and negatives in the past, we use the past tense of *do* (= *did*) + infinitive without *to*.

+	I/You/He/She/It/We/They	worked.
–	I/You/He/She/It/We/They	did not (didn't) work.
?	Did I/you/he/she/it/we/they	work?

Short answers
Yes, I/you/he/she/it/we/they **did**.
No, I/you/he/she/it/we/they **didn't**.

3 Verbs that end in *-y* change *-y* to *-ied*:
carry – **carried**

4 Verbs with one syllable ending in one vowel and one consonant, double the consonant and add *-ed*:
stop – **stopped**

5 Some verbs have irregular Past Simple forms:
*She **had** breakfast and then she **left** the house.*
See the Mini-dictionary for the past form of irregular verbs.

12.3a Time expressions with the Past Simple

Here are some time expressions with the Past Simple:

Yesterday	I **was** at home **yesterday**. Where **were** you **yesterday morning/afternoon/evening**?
Last	She **was** at the cinema **last night**. We **were** in London **last week/month/year**.

12.4 be + going to for future plans

Use

We use *be + going to* + infinitive without *to* to talk about future plans and intentions:
I'm going to have a party on my birthday.
Are you **going to visit** your family next weekend?

Form

+	I	am ('m)	going to stay at home.
	He/She/It	is ('s)	
	You/We/They	are ('re)	
−	I	am not ('m not)	going to get a new computer.
	He/She/It	is not (isn't)	
	You/We/They	are not (aren't)	
?	Am	I	going to watch the match this afternoon?
	Is	he/she/it	
	Are	you/we/they	

Short answers
Yes, **I am**. No, **I'm not**.
Yes, he/she/it **is**. No, he/she/it **isn't**.
Yes, we/you/they **are**. No, we/you/they **aren't**.

13 THERE + BE

13.1 there is/are

Use

We use *there is/are* to say that something is/is not present in a particular place:
There's a good sports centre near here.
There are twenty students in my class.
There isn't a computer room in my school.
There aren't any parks near here.

Form

+	SINGULAR	**There is** (**There's**) a café.
	PLURAL	**There are** three discos.
−	SINGULAR	**There is not** (**isn't**) a sports centre.
	PLURAL	**There are not** (**aren't**) any tennis courts.
?	SINGULAR	**Is there** a hotel near here?
	PLURAL	**Are there** any basketball courts?

Short answers
SINGULAR Yes, **there is**. No, **there isn't**.
PLURAL   Yes, **there are**. No, **there aren't**.

13.2 there was/were

Use

We use *there was/were* to say that something was/was not present in the past:
There was a good film on TV last night.
There were thirty people at his party yesterday.
There wasn't a test last week.
There weren't any pop groups at the festival.

Form

+	SINGULAR	**There was** a football match yesterday.
	PLURAL	**There were** a lot of people.
−	SINGULAR	**There was not** (**wasn't**) a film on TV.
	PLURAL	**There were not** (**weren't**) any new e-mails.
?	SINGULAR	**Was there** a tennis match?
	PLURAL	**Were there** any new students?

Short answers
SINGULAR Yes, **there was**. No, **there wasn't**.
PLURAL   Yes, **there were**. No, **there weren't**.

Pearson Education Limited
Edinburgh Gate, Harlow
Essex CM20 2JE England
and Associated Companies throughout the world.

www.longman.com

© Pearson Education Limited 2002

The right of Amanda Maris to be identified as author of this work has been asserted by her in accordance with the Copyright, Designs and Patents Act 1988.

All rights reserved; no part of this publication may be reproduced, stored in a retrieval system, or transmitted in any form or by any means, electronic, mechanical, photocopying, recording or otherwise, without the prior written permission of the copyright holders.

First published 2002
Second impression 2002
Set in ITC Officina Sans 11/13.5pt

ISBN 0582 511704

Printed in Spain by Mateu Cromo, S.A. Pinto (Madrid)

Prepared for the Publishers by Aldridge Press
www.aldridgepress.demon.co.uk

Illustrators
Jean de Lemos of GCI, Maureen and Gordon Gray

Acknowledgements
The author and publishers would like to thank the following people for their support and hard work:

John Aldridge, Robyn Alton, Paul Katumba, Elana Katz, Gülay Kiratli, Hilary Morgan, Elizabeth Paren, Teresa Pelc, Charlotte Rolfe, Lisa Rosamond, Magdalena Szewczyk, Dominika Szmerdt, Naomi Tasker, Ann Thomson, Linda Ward

Special thanks go to Naomi Tasker for her expertise, encouragement and good humour.

The author and publishers would like to thank the following people for their help in the development of this course:

Argentina: Graciela Cervera; **Colombia**: Mónica Perdomo, Lidia Gómez-Cáceres, Gloria Yamile Rodriguez, Yolima Echavez; **Poland**: Kamila Borkowska, Anna Palugniok

Photo Acknowledgements
We are grateful to the following for permission to reproduce copyright photographs:

Aldridge Press for pages 12 (centre), 24; Corel Corporation for page 59; Corbis for page 42 (left, photograph Dave G. Houser, right, photograph Ted Horowitz); Frank Fernandez for page 12 (top); The Image Bank for page 85; Images Colour Library for page 54 (centre left, photograph Duncan McEwan); Impact Photos for pages 30 (bottom, photograph Geray Sweeney), 36 (photograph Giles Barnard), 54 (centre right, photograph Martin Black), 80 (bottom, photograph Giles Barnard); Nova for pages 12 (bottom), 66; Oxford Scientific Films for page 60 (photograph Stephen Dalton); Pearson Education/Peter Lake for pages 3, 98, 99; The Photographers Library for pages 6, 30 (top), 54 (top), 80 (top); Pictures Colour Library for page 30 (centre); Still Moving Picture Company for page 54 (bottom, photograph Doug Corrance).